Adapting to Term Limits: Recent Experiences and New Directions

• • •

Bruce E. Cain
Thad Kousser

2004

Public Policy Institute of California
1994–2004

Library of Congress Cataloging-in-Publication Data
Cain, Bruce E.
Adapting to term limits : recent experiences and new directions / Bruce E. Cain
p. cm.
ISBN: 1-58213-101-5
1. California. Legislature—Term of office. 2. Legislation—California. 3. Legislative oversight—California. 4. California—Politics and government—1951- I. Kousser, Thad, 1974- II. Public Policy Institute of California. III. Title.

JK8766.C35 2004
328.794'073—dc22 2004020149

PPIC does not take or support positions on any ballot measure or on any local, state, or federal legislation, nor does it endorse, support, or oppose any political parties or candidates for public office.

Research publications reflect the views of the authors and do not necessarily reflect the views of the staff, officers, or Board of Directors of the Public Policy Institute of California.

Foreword

When political observers turn their attention to California's systemic problems, they often place term limits near the top of the list—along with the initiative process, gerrymandering, and the two-thirds requirement to pass a budget in the Legislature. Passed in 1990, Proposition 140 restricts state legislators to six years in the Assembly and eight in the Senate. Many critics argue that this restriction has harmed the legislative process. Deal-making, they maintain, is a lost art among legislators whose time horizons are compressed by term limits. Moreover, this art is required to pass a balanced budget in California. Despite these and other criticisms, term limits remain popular with voters, and few observers doubt that they are here to stay.

In this report, Bruce Cain and Thad Kousser take the discussion a step further by examining how Proposition 140 has actually affected the California Legislature. Their findings paint a mixed picture. In some ways, very little has changed. If term limit proponents hoped to curb or even banish political careerism, they have little to show for their efforts. Such careerism, the authors note, remains a constant in California politics. Although there are more female and minority representatives now than there were before the passage of Proposition 140, term limits only accelerated a process that was already under way. Legislative leaders continue to raise and allocate campaign money as they did before, and term limits have had little or no effect on the breadth or complexity of bills. In these and other ways, Proposition 140 has not radically altered the Legislature and its day-to-day operations.

Term limits have not been inconsequential, however. The authors show that the Legislature now screens fewer bills and is less likely to alter the Governor's Budget. For a variety of reasons related to term limits, there is more room for fiscal irresponsibility in the Legislature now and less incentive, experience, and leadership to correct it. Term limits also may be weakening legislative oversight of the executive branch. These changes, whether intended or not, are shifting the balance of power between the legislative and executive branches of state government.

From the authors' analyses and interviews, one message comes through loud and clear: Term limits are neither the populist victory its proponents had in mind nor the unconditional disaster some predicted it would be. Like most public policy—whether fashioned through the initiative or the legislative process—term limits have been accompanied by unintended consequences. Of these, those of most concern diminish the Legislature's capacity to perform its basic duties. Cain and Kousser do more than just identify unintended consequences and the concerns they raise. Rather, they offer several specific recommendations, one of which is to allow members 14 years of total service rather than six years in the Assembly and eight in the Senate. This change, they maintain, is consistent with the spirit of Proposition 140 but allows legislators to accrue more policy and committee experience in one or the other chamber.

Taken together, the report's recommendations suggest that modest changes in response to Proposition 140 could improve the Legislature's ability to perform its role. By proposing these changes, which grow out of their quantitative and qualitative analyses, the authors have performed a valuable service on behalf of good government in California.

David W. Lyon
President and CEO
Public Policy Institute of California

Summary

Passed in 1990, Proposition 140 changed Sacramento by setting term limits for legislators, but exactly how has it affected the Legislature, and what can the institution do to respond? This study moves beyond the stale debate over whether term limits made California politics better or worse and instead develops concrete measures of their effects and identifies ways to adapt to changes. Guided by the testimony and advice of informed observers, it offers quantitative analyses using bill histories, voting behavior, the content of bills, budget figures, and other archival records to explore how term limits have shaped the way the Legislature deals with major issues.

We find that term limits altered—but did not revolutionize—the type of legislator who comes to Sacramento. In particular, Proposition 140 helped to accelerate trends of increasing female and minority representation that were already under way in California. Instead of being a new breed of "citizen legislator," however, new members after term limits are more likely to have local government experience and to run for another office—for Assemblymembers, often a State Senate seat—when their terms expire. Careerism remains a constant in California politics.

The effects on Sacramento's policymaking processes have been more profound. In both houses, committees now screen out fewer bills assigned to them and are more likely to see their work rewritten at later stages. The practice of "hijacking" Assembly bills—gutting their contents and amending them thoroughly in the Senate—has increased sharply. As a body, the Legislature is less likely to alter the governor's budget, and its own budget process neither encourages fiscal discipline nor links legislators' requests to overall spending goals. In addition, legislative oversight of the executive branch has declined significantly. Our interviews revealed a widespread sense in Sacramento that something needs to be done soon to provide more stability and expertise to the Legislature's policymaking process. Yet there are continuities in the Legislature's internal operations as well. According to our measures, leaders remain central to the process and term limits cannot be blamed for Sacramento's intensifying partisan polarization.

Term limits have had a mixed effect on the Legislature's policy products. We observed no diminution in the breadth and complexity of bills that the Legislature passed into law, although this continuity may be the result of the Senate's increased propensity to amend Assembly bills. Using simple measures of legislative performance, we find that formal training by the C.A.P.I.T.O.L. Institute does not appear to improve a legislator's "batting average"—that is, his or her chances of passing a bill or seeing it signed into law—although legislators who receive that training tend to write shorter bills that change more code sections.[1]

Table S.1 provides a summary of our quantitative findings. Grouping our research questions into the chapters that explore them, the table includes the question we asked, the dataset we used to answer it, and the finding.

In addition to presenting these quantitative results, the report points to more general patterns emerging from our interviews and one case study. We discovered that legislators are learning more quickly than their precursors, but that frequent changes in the membership and leadership of legislative committees, especially in the Assembly, diminish their expertise and collective memory in many important policy areas. Many committees lack the experience to weed out bad bills and ensure that agencies are acting efficiently and in accordance with legislative intent. Our case study of the Quackenbush insurance investigation suggests that its success depended on the skills of specific legislators, not all of which will necessarily be preserved in a less experienced Legislature.

Another major problem area is legislative leadership. With only six years in the Assembly before a lifetime ban goes into effect, Speakers have less than two years to leave their mark, and lame duck leaders face

---

[1]The C.A.P.I.T.O.L. Institute—the acronym is short for California Assembly Program for Innovative Training and Orientation for the Legislature—teaches rules and process to new members and staff.

Table S.1

Summary of the Quantitative Findings

Research Question	Type of Data Used	Finding
Chapter 2		
Have term limits brought a new type of "citizen legislator" to Sacramento?	Career histories of all newly elected members from 1980–2000.	Today's members are more likely to come from local government and to run again when termed out.
Did Prop. 140 increase female and minority representation in the Legislature?	Records of new female and minority members and who they replaced.	Term limits sped up a diversification of the houses that was already under way.
Can new members operate effectively early in their legislative careers?	Batting averages for the Assembly classes of 1986 and 1996.	First-year performance levels and learning curves have remained constant.
Chapter 3		
Has the experience of committee chairs and the number of consultants declined?	Records from 11 major committees from 1979 to 2000.	Experience and staffing levels have declined, especially in the Assembly.
Do committees still exercise their "gatekeeping" power to screen out poor legislation?	Legislative histories of 1,920 bills over four sessions.	Gatekeeping has dropped significantly in both houses.
Do committees still amend most of the bills assigned to them?	Legislative histories of 1,920 bills over four sessions.	Yes, but amendment activity later in the process has risen greatly.
How do Assembly committees chaired by first-term members perform?	Comparisons of two committees before and after term limits.	Term limits brought a clear reduction in committee gatekeeping and amending.
Which staffing organizations suffered under Prop. 140's spending cuts?	Personnel records from each staffing organization.	Professional, nonpartisan groups bore the brunt of the cuts.

Table S.1 (continued)

Research Question	Type of Data Used	Finding
Are more bills hijacked since the implementation of term limits?	Comparison of bill records in 1993–1994 with 1997–1998.	Hijacking of Assembly bills in the Senate has nearly doubled.
How has the breadth and complexity of legislation changed?	Length and code sections affected by 988 bills over four sessions.	Term limits coincide with an increase in the breadth and complexity of bills.
Chapter 4		
Have term limits affected the tenures of top legislative leaders?	Leadership tenures since 1960.	Term limits brought instability at the top, especially in the Assembly.
What proportion of campaign contributions goes to party leaders versus committee chairs and other members?	Campaign finance records from 1986 and 1996, purged of candidate-to-candidate giving.	The distribution of money, a proxy for legislative power, remained surprisingly stable.
Are term limits to blame for the increasing polarization of legislators' voting records?	AFL-CIO scores over time for members first elected in 1986 and 1996.	Term limits have not made legislators more ideologically extreme.
Chapter 5		
Has the Legislature become weaker in budget negotiations with governors?	Line-by-line records of three budget areas over four cycles.	Term limits greatly reduced the Legislature's ability to rewrite executive proposals.
Does the Legislature still follow up its budget with requests for information from agencies?	Records of budget supplemental requests from 1985–2002.	Prop. 140 brought a sharp decline in the use of this oversight tool.
How often does the Legislature order the Bureau of State Audits to investigate agency activities?	Records of state audits ordered from 1980-2001.	The number of audits has dropped and their scope has narrowed.

Table S.1 (continued)

Research Question	Type of Data Used	Finding
Chapter 6		
Has the C.A.P.I.T.O.L. Institute prepared members to pass more legislation in their first terms?	Comparison of batting averages for the classes of 1996 and 1998.	Formal training does not appear to affect initial legislative performance.
Has the C.A.P.I.T.O.L. Institute changed the content of bills passed by members in their first terms?	Comparison of bills passed by the classes of 1996 and 1998.	Legislators who have been trained pass "cleaner" bills that are shorter but change more code sections.

serious obstacles. Special interest money still flows in roughly the same proportions to Senate and Assembly leaders and in ever rising amounts; term limits have not eased the burden of fundraising in any way. However, we find no evidence that term limits have contributed to rising legislative partisanship. New legislators are no more ideologically extreme now than they were in the past, and the longer members are in the Legislature, the more partisan they become.

Few of the most fervent hopes of Proposition 140's backers—or the worst fears of its opponents—have materialized. Even so, term limits have dramatically changed California's Legislature. Many veteran legislators and staff members regret what has happened to the institution, and the major figure behind Proposition 140 recently voiced his discontent with the results. Coping with term limits means compensating for the problems that have arisen while recognizing the value of increased turnover and legislative diversity.

With this in mind, the report makes several recommendations about training, the budget process, and modifying term limits. As relatively inexperienced legislators take on greater responsibilities, training for new members and staff plays a more critical role than ever. In particular, increased training in legislative oversight could improve the Legislature's performance in this area.

The Legislature could also ensure more stability and responsibility in the budget process by:

- Holding more joint Senate-Assembly subcommittee hearings to work out agreements in specific funding areas.
- Giving these subcommittees specific funding targets to work within.
- Reporting proposals from each house's subcommittees under closed rules so that they are not easily changed in the budget conference committee. This former practice of "locking" budget items on which both houses agreed should be reinstated to make subcommittee hearings more consequential.
- Strengthening the Legislative Analyst's Office, giving it a larger role, and staffing it at previous levels.
- Making chairs of the budget subcommittees members of the final budget conference committee to ensure that agreements made early on are adhered to more closely in the final stages.

These proposals may bring more consensus and fiscal accountability to the process.

Finally, the state should consider amending but not ending term limits. Instead of allowing legislators six years in the Assembly and eight in the Senate, a new provision could limit members to 14 years of total legislative service. This alteration would do little to erode the gains brought by Proposition 140 and would allow legislators who stay in one house to learn more about particular policy areas and committees. Experience levels for Assembly chairs and consultants, which have dropped to very low levels, would rebound. Assembly committees could also perform their gatekeeping function more proficiently. Crucially, Assembly leaders who chose not to run for the Senate would have more time to obtain expertise and lead their caucuses effectively, and the Legislature as a whole could be strengthened in its budget negotiations and oversight action. This change would make the houses more equal in experience and the branches more equal in power, even as it ensured the turnover promised by Proposition 140.

Contents

Figures

Tables

Acknowledgments

We would like to thank the legislators, staff members, lobbyists, executive officials, journalists, and other Sacramento observers we interviewed who were so generous with their time and insights. We are grateful to our many research assistants, whose contributions to the collection and analysis of data are cited throughout our report. The library staff at UC Berkeley's Institute of Governmental Studies provided us with exceptional assistance, and the preliminary work on which parts of this project are based was supported by the California Policy Research Center. Most important, drafts of this report were greatly improved by the thoughtful and detailed comments of Paul Lewis, Linda Cohen, Forrest Maltzman, Sarah Binder, Megan Mullin, Phil Isenberg, S. Karthick Ramakrishnan, Robert Naylor, Keith Hamm, and Fred Silva. Any errors are our own and any opinions or interpretations expressed in this report are ours alone and do not necessarily reflect the views of the Public Policy Institute of California.

1. Introduction

California has now had over a decade of experience with legislative term limits. All members who held office in 1990, when Proposition 140 passed, were termed out of their Assembly seats by 1996 or their Senate seats by 1998. To be sure, debates over the merits of term limits continue, but the political reality is that term limits remain popular with voters and are here to stay. Voters may eventually allow some tinkering with term length, but they are unlikely to abolish legislative term limits anytime in the near future. Hence, it seems appropriate now to document the effects that term limits have had on the California Legislature and to suggest ways in which the body might adapt.

In the early stages of term limits, academics could not easily document the rapid transformations of state legislatures. Therefore, most of the current literature focuses on how term limits affected the costs and competitiveness of elections or the demographic characteristics of their winners. As Cain and Levin (1999) note, "We tend to know more about the characteristics of pre- and post-term limit candidates than we do about the impact of term limits on legislative competence or the balance of power between the governmental branches." Because term limits in California have been in place for over a decade, these internal legislative changes can now be examined in some detail.

The question of legislative performance has never been more pressing. The electricity crisis demonstrated how technical and seemingly uncontroversial decisions can come back to haunt the state. The collapse of the dot.com industry, the economic and security issues generated by the September 2001 attack, the unsolved problems of water and transportation infrastructure, and the political upheaval brought by the recall of Governor Gray Davis are just a few of the challenges that face California government today. The California electorate has expressed a desire for high legislative turnover, but that desire has to be reconciled with its parallel expectation that government should perform competently. The challenge is to identify how best to achieve these two seemingly contradictory goals.

We attempt to break the cycle of stale debate over whether term limits have been good or bad for California government and to focus instead on measuring their actual effects and learning how to govern best under term limits. When Proposition 140 passed in 1990, the Legislature had to adapt. For legislators, this meant replacing veteran staff, finding new ways to pay for their retirement years, considering alternative career paths inside and outside politics, changing their time horizons for legislative projects, and learning to be effective in the new environment. For the institution as a whole, it meant coping with more inexperienced members, adjusting to increased turnover among its leaders, and competing with the executive branch without the institutional memory and expertise that it formerly enjoyed.

We can learn a great deal from both the observable effects of term limits and the adaptations the Legislature has already made to them. One of these adaptations is the training provided to new Assembly staff and members by the C.A.P.I.T.O.L. Institute. This report begins by presenting a variety of tests of the effects that term limits have had on the composition of the Legislature, its internal operations, and the policies that it ultimately produces. We use these findings to make policy recommendations for improving legislative functions under the constraints introduced by term limits.

Our research questions require careful collection of qualitative evidence coupled with the analysis of new quantitative data. We began in Sacramento interviewing a wide range of informed observers—including legislators, key staff members, those in the executive branch, lobbyists, and journalists—and gathering archival documents on the effects of term limits.[1]

---

[1]Our private interviews with legislative and agency staff are kept anonymous, in keeping with traditional university human subjects provisions relating to those who serve at the pleasure of elective officials. Many of our interviews with legislators are also kept anonymous, since they were conducted as part of a national term limits study in which all interviews were confidential. We worked with Karl Kurtz of the National Conference of State Legislatures to conduct many of the interviews for that project.

Until now, work on term limits has been largely descriptive and has rarely gone beyond such interviews, although Van Vecten (2001) and Clucas (2000) are notable exceptions to the pattern. Instead of stopping after this step, we use the interviews to guide the construction of four primary datasets and several smaller ones that draw on archival sources.

The four primary datasets track individual legislative performance, voting behavior, committee activity, and the breadth and complexity of bills. Each can be used to answer a variety of questions about legislative behavior after term limits. We also collect information on career histories, staffing patterns, campaign contributions, and oversight activities to answer specific questions. Focusing on the Legislature's oversight capacity in the post-term limits era, we conduct a case study, based on targeted interviews, of Insurance Commissioner Quackenbush's investigation. Finally, we assess the sum of our evidence and the Legislature's own coping strategies to offer policy recommendations.

Like most numerical summaries of complex political realities, our quantitative measures are imperfect. We do our best to explain the reasoning behind the figures and the limits of our conclusions. We realize that no single number can capture every facet of political behavior, but we feel that the flaws in any quantification are outweighed by the importance of basing our conclusions in this highly controversial realm on objective measures. When necessary, we have also attempted to ensure that the changes we observe in these measures are caused by term limits rather than by concurrent trends in redistricting, the Legislature's partisan balance, and divided government.

The remaining chapters are organized as follows. Chapter 2 examines the effect of term limits on the composition of the Legislature. In particular, it considers the role Proposition 140 played in increasing female and minority representation. It also asks whether new members are operating effectively in the early part of their legislative careers. Chapter 3 turns to legislative committees—especially to the experience levels of committee chairs and committee consultants, their ability to screen out poor legislation, and the performance of first-term committee chairs. It also examines the effects of Proposition 140 on staffing organizations, whether bills are gutted and amended more frequently as they make their way through the committee process, and the effects of term limits on the breadth and complexity of bills. Chapter 4 considers the effects of term limits on legislative leadership by examining changes in tenure, the role leaders play in fundraising before and after term limits, and whether term limits have contributed to the polarization of the major parties. Turning to relations between the legislative and executive branches, Chapter 5 investigates whether and how term limits have weakened the Legislature's position with respect to budget negotiations and oversight. Chapter 6 concludes the report by examining the Legislature's adaptations to term limits and recommending steps to minimize their less desirable consequences.

2. The Term-Limited Legislator

For the California term limits movement, the first of many goals was to change the mix of people serving in the state Legislature. Incumbency advantages, proponents argued, had undermined fair elections, preventing regular party turnover and perpetuating the political careers of professional politicians who were increasingly out of touch with the concerns of average Californians. With high name recognition and the ability to raise more money than challengers, incumbents were virtually invulnerable during the 1980s: Reelection rates for Assembly incumbents, for instance, exceeded 90 percent in the decade before Proposition 140. Representatives who retired or ran for higher office were frequently replaced by their own staff members, so that even when the faces changed, legislative perspectives often did not. Limiting Assembly and Senate terms, it was hoped, would increase the rotation into and out of office and change the background and perspectives of those serving in the Legislature.

Some supporters hoped that term limits would produce a mix of representatives that more closely resembled the general population's characteristics and attitudes: more women and minorities, fewer career politicians, fewer people obsessed with the electoral bottom line, and fewer representatives corrupted by lobbyists and party leaders. Term limit critics, on the other hand, thought it likely that post-Proposition 140 representatives would more closely resemble part-time legislators in other states—those with the leisure and wealth to serve in offices with no long-term future, few benefits, and little staff support.

Who was right? This chapter answers this question by:

- Exploring changes in the composition of California's Legislature since 1990,
- Estimating how much of the increase in the number of female and minority legislators is attributable to term limits, and

- Examining the qualitative and quantitative evidence about the experiences of term-limited members.

As proponents hoped, women and minorities have been elected to office more frequently, resulting in an increasingly diverse Legislature. Some of this transformation can be attributed to term limits, yet we also find that much of the diversification resulted from other trends that term limits merely accelerated. Our study of career histories also reveals that new members today appear to be as interested as their predecessors were in long-term political careers.

Special Elections, Turnover, and Legislator Backgrounds

When Proposition 140 was enacted in November 1990, state representatives holding office at that time were allowed to serve their full terms, regardless of their previous length of service. Thus, it took six years in the Assembly and eight years in the Senate to replace the membership of each house. The effects of the initiative, then, can be thought of as unfolding over three stages. The first was from 1990 to 1995, as legislators anticipated the effects of term limits and often began planning their next career moves. The second stage, in the late 1990s, saw a flood of new members enter and transform each house, especially the Assembly. The third stage, which will begin with the November 2004 elections, removes veteran legislators who served the maximum terms in both houses.

Between 1990 and 1995, the normal turnover cycle was accelerated modestly by the early departures of legislators who pursued opportunities for higher office or private sector employment. California's state legislators, who have always aspired to Congressional seats and other positions, are emboldened by constitutional provisions that allow them to move up while holding or running for legislative seats. Faced with term limits, many left their seats and thereby created the need for special elections. Before 1990, the number of special elections typically fell in the range of one to four seats, with a large spike in 1973 after the court-controlled Special Masters' redistricting (Figure 2.1).[1] After 1990, there were at least four special elections every year except one from 1990 to 1995. After 1995, California returned to a more normal pattern of special elections, but this short burst following the implementation of term limits accelerated compositional changes in the Legislature (Lee, 2001).

Death was the major cause of special elections in 1973, accounting for half of the special elections (Figure 2.2). By contrast, the death of an incumbent accounted for only one special election in 1991 and 1993 combined. Rather, most special elections were caused by incumbents resigning, being elected or appointed to other offices, or pursuing other job prospects. This pattern suggests that term limits gave rise to more special elections.

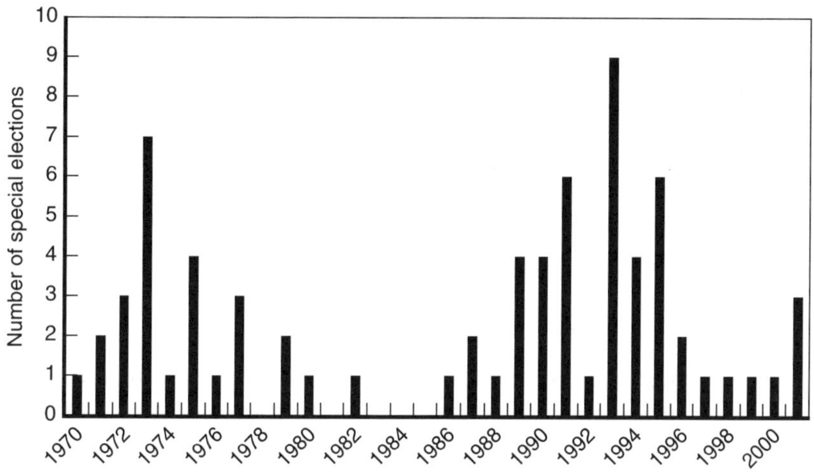

Data collected from Secretary of State Elections Division records by Anka Lee.

Figure 2.1—Frequency of Special Elections, 1970–2001

---

[1]The work of another group of Special Masters is also important to consider here. In November 1991, the Special Masters on Reapportionment filed a report with recommendations for new districts for the Legislature, Congress, and the Board of Equalization. They drew the districts to comply with the Voting Rights Act.

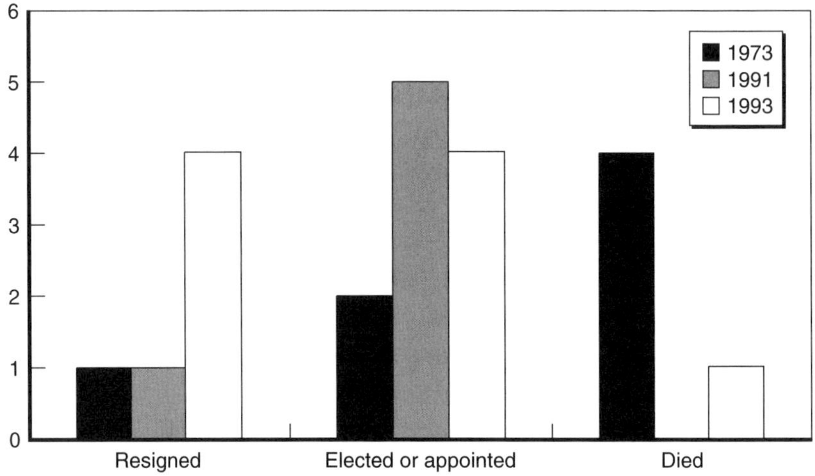

Data collected from Secretary of State Elections Division records by Anka Lee.

Figure 2.2—Reasons Incumbents Leave Office

No one seriously contested the idea that term limits would increase legislative turnover, which rose from 84 new legislators in the 1980s to 160 in the 1990s. But critics suggested that the prospect of shortened office terms combined with cuts to legislative pensions and staff support would make the job less appealing to young, ambitious, and less affluent candidates. That did not happen.

On average, California state legislators are younger now than they were before Proposition 140 passed. Specifically, the average age of new members has dropped from 47 to 42 (Barge, 2001). There is some difference between men and women, with women more likely to enter the Legislature at an older age after raising their families. Several female legislators we interviewed suggested that this gap created a difference in the perspectives of male and female legislators, influencing both how they worked and their legislative interests. However, the Legislature has not become a home for private sector retirees, as some critics predicted.

Women's Representation

The dramatic increase in the number of women and minorities elected to the Legislature in the 1990s also seemed to vindicate proponents of term limits. How much of this dramatic increase was caused by term limits and how much by other factors? When Proposition 140 was passed and implemented, California's demographics were changing, its districts were being redrawn, and organizations such as the Legislature's Latino Caucus and the national women's group EMILY's List became more active.[2] Disentangling the effects of term limits from these trends is a difficult but not hopeless task. Much can be learned about the gains of women and minorities by looking closely at the timing of these gains, the legislators who were replaced, and parallel patterns in California's Congressional delegation.

From 1972 to 1990, women's representation climbed slowly. An average of two new Assemblywomen were elected every two years and one new female State Senator every four years. Since 1990, that representation has increased dramatically, with eight new Assemblywomen per two-year cycle and five new women per four-year cycle in the Senate. Before attributing all of this increase to term limits, however, we should note the timing of the large surges. Much of this increase occurred in 1992, often dubbed the "Year of the Woman" (Figure 2.3). Four years before Proposition 140 brought its first set of forced retirements, 15 women were elected to the two houses. National events likely increased the propensity of high-quality female candidates to run, and the 1991 Special Masters' redistricting gave them the opportunity by creating many open seats.

After dropping in 1994, the number of new female legislators grew sharply, bringing in 28 new Assemblywomen and 11 new female Senators. Whom did they replace? From 1996 to 2001, 71 percent of the new Assemblywomen replaced a term-limited member, 25 percent replaced someone who ran for another office, and only one (Wilma

---

[2]Noting that Democrats had great electoral success during the 1996, 1998, and 2000 elections, one reviewer of this report observed that this success should lead to the election of more female and minority legislators, who tend to be Democrats.

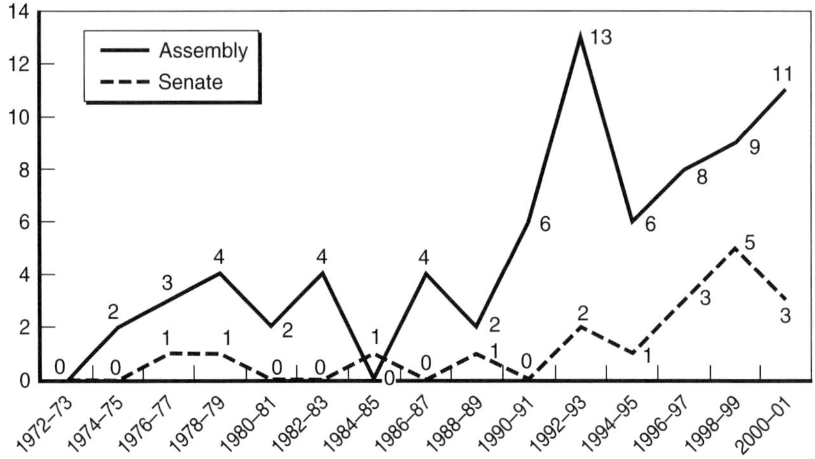

Data collected from election records and rosters by Kelly Yang.

Figure 2.3—Women Newly Elected to the Assembly and Senate, 1972–2001

Chan) defeated an incumbent. This pattern contrasts with that of the 1990–1995 period, when 23 percent beat an incumbent, 23 percent replaced an incumbent who retired or died, and 27 percent won a new seat created by redistricting. The remaining 27 percent replaced a member running for another office, probably in anticipation of term limits. Using this calculus, we estimate that 18 of the 25 Assemblywomen newly elected from 1990 to 1995 did not owe their victory to term limits. Over the next three elections, 27 Assemblywomen won seats that were directly or indirectly vacated as a result of term limits. Comparing these figures indicates that term limits opened up nine Assembly seats for women over the course of three elections (Yang, 2002).

Minority Representation

A similar story can be told about black, Latino, and Asian American representation in the Legislature. The dramatic increase in minority legislators was ultimately the product of underlying demographic change. California's Latino and Asian American populations grew dramatically in the 1980s and 1990s. Because much of this growth came from immigration, its political implications were delayed; foreign-born residents had to become naturalized and then active in the political system. In a conscientious attempt to comply with the Voting Rights Act, the 1991 Special Masters' redistricting created many more so-called majority-minority districts—that is, districts in which Latinos, especially, constituted a majority of the voting-age, eligible population. From 1990 to 1995, 17 new minority Assemblymembers and four new minority State Senators were elected to office, primarily because of redistricting.[3] When term limits took effect between 1996 and 2001, minority gains rose to 33 new members in the Assembly and nine in the Senate.

Again, we review whom these new members replaced to estimate how much of the effect can be attributed to term limits. In the early 1990s, 11 of the 17 newly elected minority members won their seats for reasons not linked to term limits. After term limits, 15 percent of new members beat an incumbent or replaced a retiree, but 85 percent (28) took seats opened up by term limits. By this measure, term limits resulted in 17 new minority legislators.

However, term limits removed minority legislators at the same time that they opened up seats. During the 1990s, ten women and 19 minority legislators were termed out, and the loss of such members as Willie Brown was costly for the influence and expertise of minority legislators. The net effect of Proposition 140 can be seen more clearly by looking at total numbers of minorities in the Legislature rather than by focusing only on newly elected members. During the 1990s, the number of Latino and Asian American members grew as the number of white and black legislators declined (Figures 2.4 and 2.5). Blacks held nine seats in the two houses when Proposition 140 was passed but hold only six today. The impressive gains of Latinos reached their apex in 2000 and dropped in 2002.

---

[3]To count minority legislators, we first relied on directories that included photographs. Although this was sufficient to count the number of black and Asian American officials, gauging Latino representation was often difficult. We therefore used supplemental information such as Latino caucus membership, official biographies, lists provided by ethnic organizations, and press coverage to make final determinations. We did not count those with Portuguese heritage as Latinos.

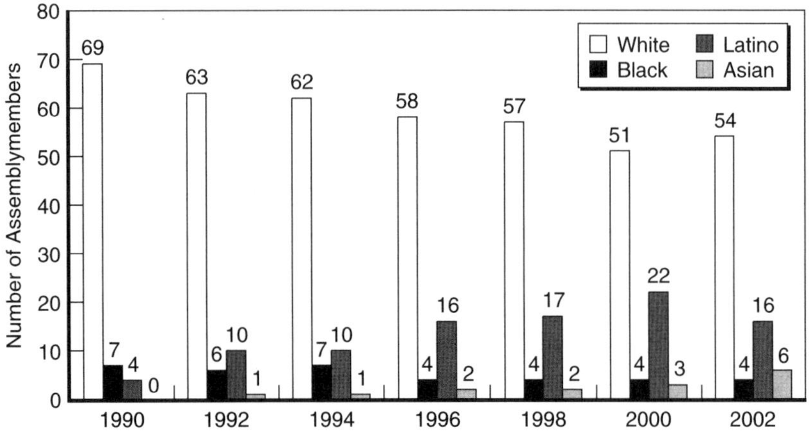

Data collected from appropriate editions of the California Journal's *Roster and Government Guide.*

Figure 2.4—Racial and Ethnic Composition of the California Assembly, 1990–2002

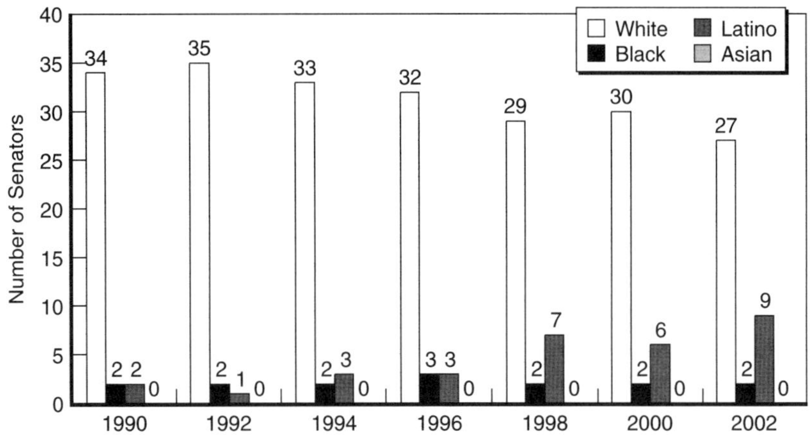

Data collected from appropriate editions of the California Journal's *Roster and Government Guide.*

Figure 2.5—Racial and Ethnic Composition of the California Senate, 1990–2002

We seek to isolate the effects of term limits on the composition of California's Legislature by comparing trends in the Assembly and Senate to those in the state's Congressional delegation. Members of Congress do not face term limits.[4] From 1990 to 2000, the share of state legislative seats held by women grew from 19.2 percent to 29.2 percent. Over the same period, the percentage of women in California's House seats rose from 6.7 percent to 30.8 percent. In 1992, Californians also elected Senators Barbara Boxer and Dianne Feinstein. This analysis suggests that term limits have not been responsible for any of the increase in women's representation.

Although the number of minority members in the Congressional delegation has grown (Figure 2.6), the shift has not been as great as that in Sacramento. We give these figures perspective by comparing the composition of California's population to the breakdown of its state and

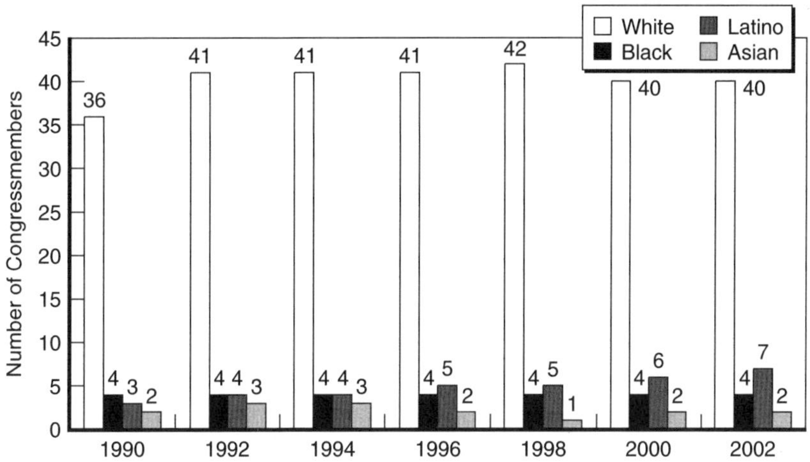

Data collected from Green (1991), *Congressional Quarterly's Who's Who in Congress* (various years), and Barone and Cohen (2003) by Matt Tokeshi.

Figure 2.6—Racial and Ethnic Composition of California's Congressional Delegation, 1990–2002

---

[4]Although Proposition 140 was intended to apply to California's Congressional delegation, the U.S. Supreme Court ruled in its 1995 *U.S. Term Limits, Inc. v. Thornton* decision that states could not limit the terms of their federal representatives.

federal representatives in 1990 and 2000. According to the 1990 census, 26 percent of Californians were "Hispanic." Only 6.7 percent of its U.S. House members and 5 percent of its state legislators were Latino. Asian and Pacific Islanders made up 9.3 percent of the population but held 4.4 percent of House seats and no state legislative districts. With 7 percent of the state's residents, blacks held 8.9 percent of U.S. House seats and 7.5 percent of state seats. Minority representatives did better in Congressional races than they did in state contests.

By the 2000 census, Latinos accounted for 32.4 percent of the state's population, 11.5 percent of its Congressional delegation, and 23.3 percent of its state legislators. Asian and Pacific Islanders had grown to 11.2 percent of residents, had stalled at 3.8 percent of U.S. Representatives, but had taken 5 percent of the seats in the Legislature. Blacks, with 6.4 percent of the population, held 7.7 percent of Congressional seats and 5 percent of state districts.[5] For Latinos and Asians, whose numbers were rapidly growing over this period, term limits seem to have made seats in Sacramento more attainable than positions in Washington. Yet for blacks, whose share of the population shrank, term limits left the gains of the 1970s and 1980s vulnerable at a time when Congressional seats provided safe havens.

Although term limits proponents can claim some credit for diversifying the Legislature, they did not predict other trends as accurately. To begin with, term limits did not lessen political careerism. The number of new members who were former legislative staffers dropped from 40 percent in the 1980s to 16 percent in the 1990s, but the percentage of local officeholders who won legislative seats increased from 52 percent to 64 percent. In other words, local officeholders and candidates from the private sector were the primary beneficiaries of the new opportunities created by term limits. Given the expense of running for office in California's large legislative districts, it was difficult for inexperienced, less affluent candidates to win legislative seats in large numbers.

---

[5]The analysis of the 1990 census data comes from the Department of Finance (1999), and we have not reported the Native American population percentage. The analysis of 2000 census data comes from the Department of Finance (2003), and we have not reported American Indian or mixed-race population percentages.

In the term limits era, a lengthy political career requires changing offices more frequently. A common career path now is from a local office (e.g., city council, board of supervisors, special district, or school board) to the Assembly, then to the Senate, and finally to higher office or back down to local government. Although few elected officials return to local government, this path is chosen more frequently now than it was before term limits, and the effects of this pattern are potentially important.

Even within the Legislature, the career path of the post-term limit legislator has changed over time. In 1961, only a fifth of the Senate had served in the Assembly (Figure 2.7). The cultures of the two houses could remain distinct because few legislators had served in both of them. By the 1980s, when careerism became the norm, the share of Senators who had been Assemblymembers had risen to 65 percent. By 2001, that figure rose to 90 percent. Instead of staying longer in one house, the successful legislator is now more likely to serve in both houses. As a result of this new pattern, the State Assembly and Senate now have very

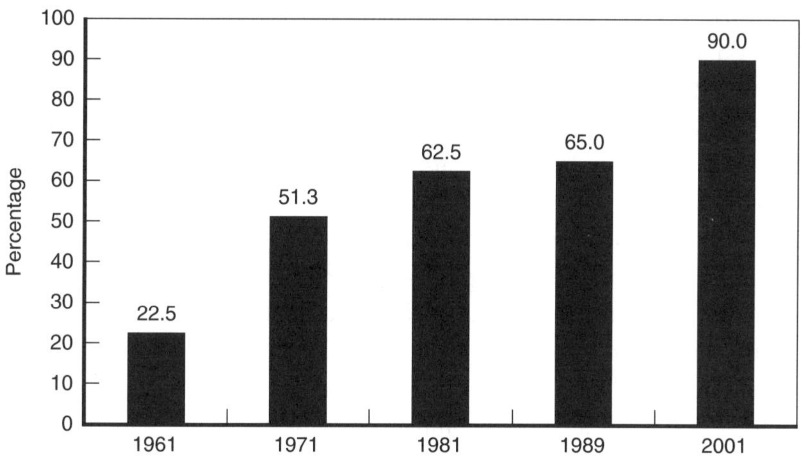

Data collected from Senator biographies published in *The California Blue Book* (1950, 1954, and 2000) and *The Little Black Book of the California Legislature* (1961, 1971, 1981, and 1989) by Brian Brokaw.

Figure 2.7—Senators with Assembly Experience, as a Percentage of Senate Membership

different experience levels. Most Senators have served at least one term in the Assembly, whereas most Assemblymembers come out of local government. This fact underlies some of our later findings, which indicate that the more experienced Senate tends to override Assembly action by amendment and legislative maneuvering more often in the post-term limits era.

Adjusting to the State Legislature

How do new members adapt to the Legislature? To answer this question, we asked some members how they learned to do their jobs in Sacramento. All members elected after term limits mentioned how much they had to learn when they arrived. This is not a new phenomenon, but legislators now face greater pressure to take on bigger roles more quickly. (One who said, "I sat and listened for the first two years," was more patient than most.) Members first must learn the process, including the basics of writing and passing legislation as well as procedure on the floor and committees. Most seemed to feel that this information could be mastered reasonably quickly, but that acquiring policy and budget expertise took much more time, and that learning how to deal effectively with colleagues and lobbyists took even longer.

The C.A.P.I.T.O.L. Institute teaches rules and process fairly well, but learning how to be effective usually requires mentoring from more experienced colleagues. As one Assemblywoman explained, the formal classes do not teach "what makes this place run." No one explained, for example, that "when you accept an opponent's amendment, it does not mean that they are now neutral or that their opposition is removed." Rather, she found out the hard way that "many members will demand amendments and then continue to vote against your bill." It also takes time, she said, to learn about complex policy areas and the state budget. The state's water policy, for instance, affects her district, and she has tried hard to master it. In the end, however, she concluded that she would "need ten years to learn enough to make a difference." Despite seven years of local government budget experience, she also found the state budget complex and overwhelming. As another member put it, "I felt like I was just beginning to become an effective member at the end of my third term in the Assembly."

From whom do members learn? For political advice, they rely most heavily on their more experienced peers. Female legislators, we were told, tend to rely more on other female legislators. New legislators also learn from experienced staff. Several members spoke to us about the value of having staff with "in-the-building experience," meaning staff who had served for other legislators or for committees. Some new members made the mistake of recruiting their legislative staff exclusively from the ranks of their campaign staff. The problem with that strategy, they discovered, is that their staff "didn't even know how to collect the mail, let alone draft complex legislation."

Many legislators turned to lobbyists for guidance. A few new members confessed that in their first year, over 90 percent of their bills were drafted or given to them by lobbyists. When members had questions that their staff and other members could not answer, they called lobbyists for explanations. Although consulting with lobbyists is not a new practice in the California Legislature, some interviewees told us that since term limits were implemented, members have relied more on lobbyists to craft bills.

New members must also adjust to the intense partisanship of the Legislature. Many come out of nonpartisan local government, ill prepared for the way that party lines divide the Legislature. This was particularly true for the Republican members who discovered that their opinions were ignored from the start because of their party affiliation.

New members are on a faster career timetable, and this seems to affect the way they operate as legislators. Twenty years ago, legislators could not hold leadership positions until they had served a few terms in office. Now even freshman legislators can aspire to powerful positions. Long-serving legislators are very critical of this aspect of term limits. Yearning for the days when legislators listened and learned, one senior Democratic legislator claimed that new members come to Sacramento with an "artificial urgency" created by term limits to "get things done when they get here." This often means that there are "people screaming rather than listening." Moreover, "they don't understand the complexity of problems" and lack the time "to build the networks of people who can inform you on the issues." Another experienced legislator who had served since the 1980s said that the new members were quite talented, but that "they are not given the opportunity to grow." As a result, what happens in the Legislature "no longer matters, because big problems are not solved here." Other senior staff complained that new legislators "have shorter time horizons" and are "too willing to take short cuts for the sake of expediency." On the other hand, one legislator who was elected after 1990 and was soon to be termed out acknowledged that she "wouldn't have had nearly the career in the Legislature" that she had without term limits. A former Assembly Speaker argued that for all the complaints, the Legislature "never had brighter legislators than it does today." Furthermore, this former Speaker maintained, it was a myth that "you can't make deals anymore."

We found the testimony about the net value of term limits to be mixed. No one seems to dispute that legislative life has changed significantly. New legislators must learn faster, take more responsibility sooner, and operate with fewer personal relationships than legislators in the past.

Whether they are more effective is the subject of some dispute. One very simple measure of effectiveness is the ability to have their bills passed. To gauge this ability, we compiled "batting averages" for the classes of new Assemblymembers first elected in 1986 and 1996 (Figures 2.8 and 2.9). Batting averages represent a crude measure of legislative effectiveness but provide an objective way to compare the performances of many members across sessions.[6] We chose 1986 and 1996 because they are years in which Democrats controlled the Legislature and Republicans controlled the governor's office. Figure 2.8 details the average percentage of bills that were enrolled (passed both houses of the Legislature), whereas Figure 2.9 reports the mean percentages of bills that were chaptered (became law). We track the members of each class in their first, second, and third terms, and break them into groups—first by party and then by gender.

The data yield several conclusions. First, the overall hit rate has not dropped as a result of term limits. On average, legislators pass slightly more than half their bills in their first few terms, and just under half are

---

[6]This measure of legislative effectiveness and its drawbacks are discussed at length in Kousser (2002a).

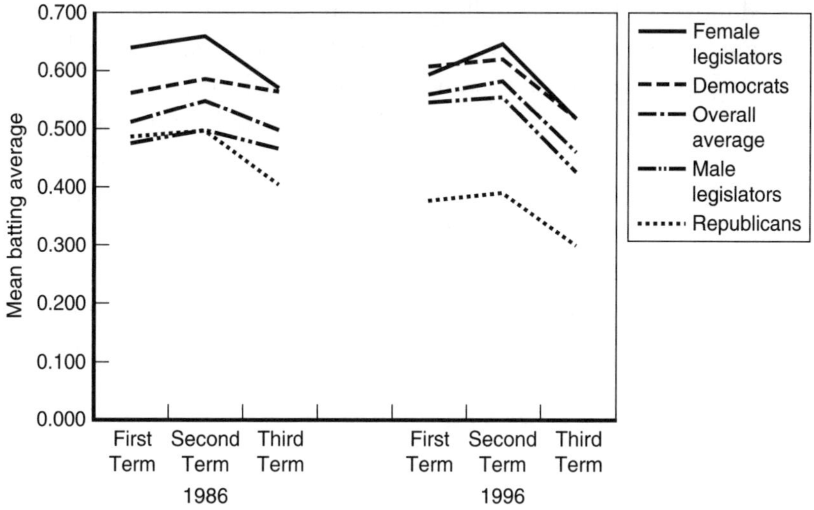

Data collected from bill histories by Cathy Ellis and Tam Bui.

Figure 2.8—Mean Batting Averages for the Classes of 1986 and 1996, Enrolled Bills

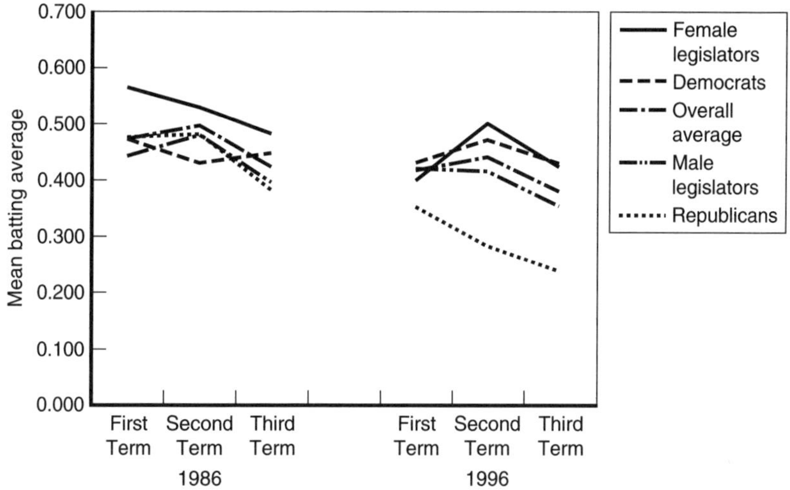

Data collected from bill histories by Cathy Ellis and Tam Bui.

Figure 2.9—Mean Batting Averages for the Classes of 1986 and 1996, Chaptered Bills

signed into law. In both enrolling and chaptering rates, there is a sophomore surge followed by a decline in the third term. This decline is sharper for the class of 1996, whose members faced term limits. It is difficult to determine whether this decline is because legislators are more willing to author controversial legislation late in their Assembly careers or because they are lame ducks. In general, however, term limits have not dramatically altered the average legislative output of new members or their pattern of performance.

A few secondary effects become clear when we analyze groups of legislators. First, the figures validate the perception that Republicans have been less powerful in the term limits era. The gap in party performance is much larger for the class of 1996 than it was for the class of 1986, with third term Republican legislators now turning less than a quarter of their bills into law. This is consistent with patterns in three other term-limited states. Finally, the data reveal that women have been more effective legislators than men, although this pattern also reflects the fact that more of the women are Democrats.

Conclusion

Neither critics nor proponents of term limits perfectly predicted their consequences. Term limits resulted in more diversity among new members but no less careerism. The new members do not look like part-time legislators in other states; rather, they resemble the ambitious young professional politicians that California has produced for three decades. The new Legislature is highly partisan, very demanding in terms of what new members must learn, and thrusts responsibility upon them very early. They are mastering the process quickly with the help of staff and lobbyists, but their policy focus is more short-term and less expert in many instances.

3. The Policymaking Process and Its Products

Proponents and critics alike predicted that term limits would change the process by which policy was crafted and thereby affect the legislation that the body ultimately produced. This chapter examines the effects of term limits on the process and products of the California Legislature.

We begin with committees, the central agents for evaluating and shaping legislation. By examining committee rosters, we show how much term limits have reduced the experience levels of chairs and their key staff members. We also comb through legislative histories of nearly 2,000 bills to see if this diminution in experience alters committee behavior. We find a dramatic drop in gatekeeping, the process by which committees screen out poorly crafted or unpopular legislation to allow the general membership to focus on a smaller set of bills. Since 1990, committees have killed far fewer bills, and amendments are more common, especially when Senate committees with experienced members hear Assembly bills. This pattern suggests that Assembly committees are passing legislation that is far from finished. Combining our data on committee experience levels with committee behavior figures, we find that Assembly committees with new chairs have been most acutely affected by term limits. Specifically, they perform their screening and shaping duties much less often after term limits.

Committees are not the only parts of the policymaking process that have been affected by term limits. In a move that seems to contradict the intentions of Proposition 140, the Legislature has accepted sharp cuts in the expert staffs that served legislators of both parties. Term limits also appear to have encouraged a much-criticized shift in the overall legislative process—an increase in the number of bills that are gutted of their content and amended thoroughly so as to escape a full set of hearings.

How have these changes altered the legislation that is produced? To answer this key question, we present a large-scale quantitative analysis of the breadth and complexity of legislation. Surprisingly, we find that chaptered bills have become broader and more complex since the advent of term limits.

Committee Experience and Behavior

Although committees in the California Legislature have never been quite as powerful or as specialized as those in the U.S. Congress, they remain the primary policymaking venues in Sacramento. Committees hear every piece of legislation that moves through each house.[1] Busy legislators often rely on written analyses, assembled by committee consultants, that summarize a bill's contents, its history, arguments for and against passage, and the interest groups who have registered formal support or opposition. Policy and fiscal committees are the most likely graveyards of legislation. When a committee does pass a bill, it frequently amends its content to make it more palatable to the chairs or membership. Committees make themselves central to the process by examining legislation, screening out unpopular bills, altering others, and framing the debate through their analyses of anything they allow to progress to the next stage.

Have term limits altered the role of committees in Sacramento? We investigate this question first by examining the most obvious way in which Proposition 140 changed committees: by removing veteran chairs and spurring turnover among the expert staff members. We then look at changes in such behaviors as gatekeeping and amendment activity and finally explore the link between a particular committee's experience levels and its actions.

---

[1]The requirement that committees grant a hearing to any author who wants one—and conduct a roll call vote whenever a motion to do so is seconded—makes California's committees less powerful procedurally than those in Congress and in most other state legislatures. Without the chair's "pocket veto," committees in California move a higher percentage of bills out of committee and provide more opportunities for the minority party and majority mavericks to pass legislation.

Experience Levels of Committee Chairs and Staff

No one doubted that Proposition 140 would reduce the tenures of committee chairs, but its other effects have been less clear. One argument suggests that Proposition 140 creates new incentives to jump from committee to committee to move up Sacramento's power ladder quickly. Another possibility is that, as detailed policy knowledge becomes especially rare and valuable, party leaders encourage new members to become specialists and move them up a particular committee's ladder on an accelerated schedule. In this case, we should see new members become chairs quickly and remain there for most of their terms.

In this section, we test these conflicting accounts by examining committee records before and after term limits. In particular, we measure the average tenure of chairs, the length of their apprenticeship on their committees, their previous length of service in the Legislature, and how much staff assistance they have been given. We present separate figures from each house to test the conventional wisdom that most committee expertise now resides in the Senate. We find that the differing effects of term limits on each house have led to vastly different levels of committee and staff expertise. Although these figures show that there is less committee expertise in the post-term limits Legislature overall, each house's adaptation strategies have led to more continuity than one might expect under term limits.

Our figures come from five key policy committees in the Senate and six parallel bodies in the Assembly, tracked over 11 sessions.[2] We computed average experience levels for all committees in three periods: 1979–1990, before term limits were part of California law; 1991–1996, after Proposition 140 had passed but before it was broadly implemented; and 1997–2000, after many veteran members had been termed out.

---

[2]In the Senate, our sample includes the Judiciary, Education, Health and Human Services, Industrial Relations/Labor, and Agriculture Committees. In the Assembly, our sample includes the Judiciary, Education, Health, Human Services, and Industrial Relations/Labor and Employment Committees. Committee membership, legislative tenure, and previous occupations were gathered from committee rosters, appropriate issues of the *California Journal*, and the *California Blue Book* by research assistant Brian Brokaw.

Before term limits, the experience levels of Senate and Assembly chairs were nearly identical (Figure 3.1). At the beginning of each session from 1979 to 1990, Senate chairs had already served an average of 5.6 years; the comparable figure for Assembly chairs was 5.7 years. After the passage of Proposition 140, veteran Senators remained in control of their committees, but Assembly chair tenures dropped dramatically. We hesitate to attribute any of this effect to term limits, however, because it can also be explained by the Republican takeover of the Assembly in 1995–1996. When Republicans finally consolidated their power under Speaker Curt Pringle in early 1996, Republican chairs replaced longtime Democratic committee chiefs. Although some of this effect certainly carries over into the post-term limits era, the pattern that we observe from 1996 will likely be typical of the near future. The average Senate chair serves about as long as a Senate term, 4.2 years, and the mean tenure of Assembly chairs (2.5 years) is slightly longer than one Assembly term. Although there have been some notable exceptions, such as Carole Migden spending her entire Assembly career running the powerful Appropriations Committee, most majority-party members appear to spend no more than a single term atop committees.

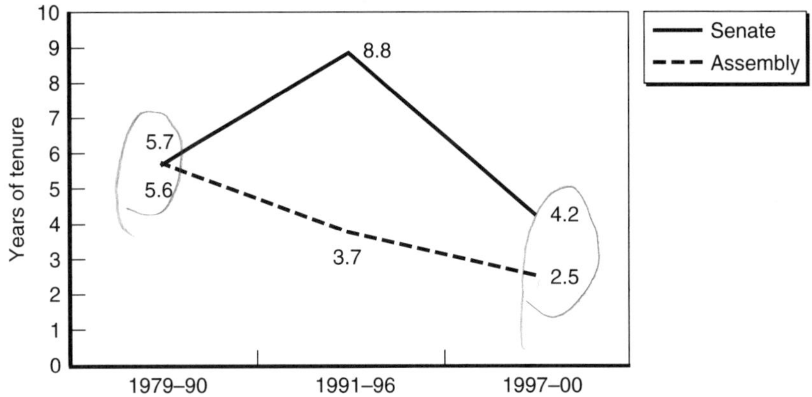

Data collected from committee rosters, appropriate issues of the *California Journal*, and the *California Blue Book* by research assistant Brian Brokaw.

Figure 3.1—Average Tenure of Committee Chairs

Figure 3.2 looks at members' apprenticeship on committees before they became chairs. Before term limits, Assemblymembers spent almost three times as much time on committees as Senators before ascending to the chair slot, although neither apprenticeship was as long as Sacramento lore might suggest. Since the passage of Proposition 140, this gap has narrowed. Neither house now requires its chairs to spend much more than a session on a committee before becoming chair, further evidence that legislators now rotate between committees rather than specialize in one policy area.[3]

A major difference between the houses is revealed by Figure 3.3, which tracks chairs' levels of previous experience in either house of the Legislature. Although the houses did not differ much in this regard before term limits, they have diverged since then. Today, Senate chairs have had nearly four times as much time as their Assembly counterparts to learn the general lessons of California politics and policy. It appears that the Assembly has attempted to compensate for this difference by

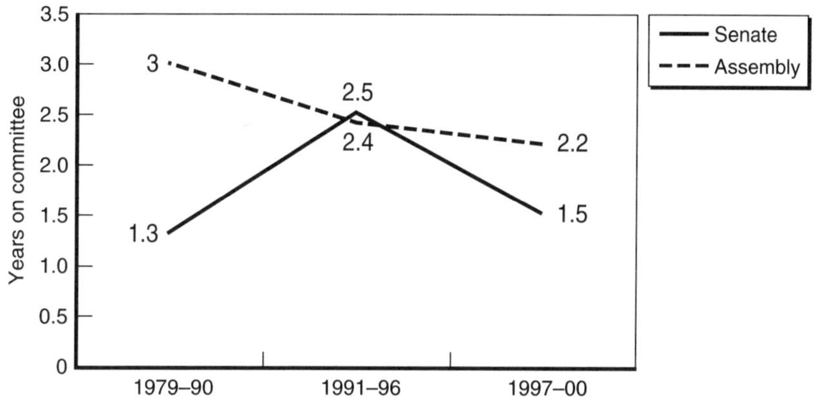

Data collected from committee rosters, appropriate issues of the *California Journal*, and the *California Blue Book* by research assistant Brian Brokaw.

Figure 3.2—Average Service of Chairs on Committee

[3]This finding is especially surprising given that legislators in both houses typically serve on two to four standing committees, with some serving on as many as six. Even with the opportunity to specialize in multiple areas, some chairs take over a committee on which they have never served.

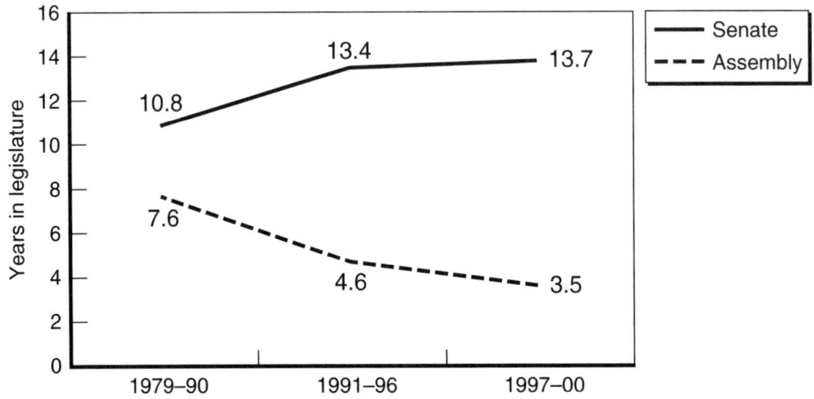

Data collected from committee rosters, appropriate issues of the *California Journal*, and the *California Blue Book* by research assistant Brian Brokaw.

Figure 3.3—Chairs' Prior Tenure in the Legislature

appointing chairs who bring outside experience relevant to the committee's domain. For instance, Assembly Health Chair Martin Gallegos (1997–2000) was a chiropractor, and Assembly Judiciary Chairs Martha Escutia (1997–1998) and Sheila Kuehl (1999–2000) were attorneys. Still, some members argue that this is no substitute for Sacramento experience. One veteran Senator describes serving in the Assembly for 15 years before serving as a committee chair: "Now, new legislators have to ramp up fast. They have to find a mentor, learn who they can trust. There is no time to listen and learn."[4]

Finally, we examine staffing patterns. Because of Proposition 140's budget cuts, the Legislature reduced the number of its committee consultants. Generally more professional and less partisan than personal staff, these consultants provide policy expertise at a moment's notice.[5] The total number of consultants and the number assigned to each committee declined sharply after Proposition 140, although staffing

[4]Interview by Karl Kurtz, Sacramento, California, February 27, 2002.

[5]"Professional" staff generally refers to those who have made staffing their career, possess relevant professional degrees or work experience, and in many cases (although not in the case of committee consultants) do not serve at the pleasure of legislators.

levels have begun to increase again to levels near those of the pre-term limits era (Figure 3.4).

In the Senate especially, leaders have strongly encouraged members to retain existing committee consultants to preserve policy expertise. One Senator we interviewed has chaired three committees in the Senate and kept the previous policy staff each time. "I probably would not have been made the chair if I had said that I wanted to change the staff," she explained.[6] By contrast, new Assembly chairs have more freedom to alter committee staffs. An Assemblymember told us that when he became the Assembly Public Safety Committee Chair, he was not required to keep the existing committee staff, although he chose to do so.[7]

The Senate has begun to institutionalize this policy as well as other practices to cope with term limits. In the Senate, new chairs receive a letter advising them that that committee staff are not to be removed for six months, and that only one consultant is to be removed at that time.

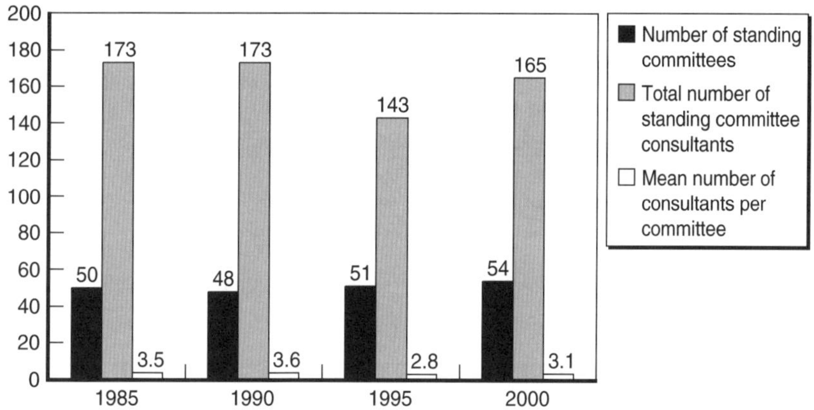

Data collected from committee staff rosters by Cathy Ellis.

Figure 3.4—Number of Committee Consultants in the California Legislature, 1985–2000

---

[6]Interview by Karl Kurtz, Sacramento, California, February 26, 2002.

[7]Interview by Karl Kurtz and Thad Kousser, Sacramento, California, February 28, 2002.

The Secretary of the Senate's office is active in soliciting senior staff to work for new members.[8] An examination of the tenures of committee staff in each house shows that these differing practices have had a clear effect. Brokaw, Jobson, and Vercruyssen (2001) find that the average tenure of chief consultants to the Assembly's standing committees declined from 8.7 years to 4 years from 1989 to 2000, whereas tenures in the Senate rose from 5.3 years in 1990 to 7.8 years in 2000. Records also show that the most experienced consultants in the Senate were matched up with the more junior chairs.

Committee Gatekeeping and Amendment Activity

> There has been an essential evisceration of the hearing process. . . . Nothing dies anymore, and there are no rules.
>
> — Former Senator who chaired various committees and served in the executive branch.[9]

> Since term limits, there is less scrutiny of legislation and less quality in both houses, but a much steeper decline in the Assembly.
>
> — Senate committee consultant.[10]

> You don't have the trust and give-and-take between members of the different parties that went along with long experience. . . . Term limits weakened Speakers, and brought more partisan but more congenial relationships, and so no one wants to kill each other's bills.
>
> — Assembly committee consultant.[11]

Nearly every legislator and Sacramento observer has a theory about how committees have changed and why. Many say that committees have abdicated their responsibility to screen out poor legislation,

---

[8]Telephone interview by Thad Kousser, June 19, 2001.

[9]Interview by Karl Kurtz and Thad Kousser, Sacramento, California, February 25, 2002.

[10]Interview by Thad Kousser, Sacramento, California, July 24, 2001.

[11]Telephone interview by Thad Kousser, August 2001. "Consent" refers to the consent calendars that the floors and some committees use to pass uncontroversial bills in bulk.

although the reasons given for this change differ. One explanation is that inexperienced members are reluctant to risk making an enemy by voting against legislation authored by a friendly face. Another is that because term-limited members will not be around very long, they will not have to pay the future costs of passing misguided bills. Another common observation about committee behavior is that amendments are less frequent and less thoughtful. The reasons offered are a lack of experience among chairs, committee staff, and committee members as well as shortened time horizons.

To test these observations, we collected records of how committees have treated thousands of bills over the past two decades that we randomly sampled. These records indicate whether a piece of legislation came up for a vote in committee, detail the results of the vote, show whether the bill was amended, and report the bill's subsequent history. They are taken from Assembly and Senate Final Histories for the relevant sessions. Although these records omit important information about bills and their histories, they are the best sources that we have for the systematic examination of committee behavior.

We looked at bills heard in four parallel committees in the Senate and Assembly: the Judiciary, Natural Resources, Labor, and Education Committees. For each committee in each session, we drew a random sample of bills and traced their histories.[12] The sessions that we examined—1979–1980, 1987–1988, 1997–1998, and 1999–2000—represent two matching pairs before and after term limits.[13] We observe

[12]Our sampling scheme ensured that each bill heard by one of the four committees during a given session had an equal chance of being drawn into our sample. This makes our sample representative of the actions of each committee, although not necessarily of the entire Legislature; the committees that hear more bills are not given more weight. We chose this method to enable valid inferences on a committee-by-committee basis. Because we use the same committees across time, and committee workloads do not shift much, this strategy does not bias our analysis of the effects of term limits.

[13]Although we cannot be certain that differences we observe between each pair of sessions are due entirely to term limits, we have tried to "control for" other factors by matching sessions that are as similar as possible in other political conditions, conducting analyses of four sessions over 20 years to guard against a one-session fluke, and comparing our findings with those of other researchers in states with and without term limits. These findings are part of a study organized by the National Conference of State Legislatures and the Council of State Governments.

the effects of Proposition 140 on committee actions when control of California government was divided between the two parties by comparing records from 1987–1988 to those from 1997–1998. In the 1987–1988 meetings, Democrats held eight-seat majorities in both the Assembly and the Senate, but they were forced to negotiate with Republican Governor George Deukmejian, who vetoed 603 bills during the session. A decade later, Democrats still had a six-seat edge in the Assembly and a seven-seat lead in the Senate and still dealt with a Republican governor, Pete Wilson, who used his veto pen 548 times during the two years.

To see how term limits affected committees during eras of unified government, we contrast the 1979–1980 and 1999–2000 sessions. In the first session, when Jerry Brown was governor, his fellow Democrats held 50 of the Assembly's 80 seats and 25 of the 40 Senate seats. By the time Democrats next captured the governor's office with Gray Davis' election in November 1998, the party controlled 48 Assembly and 25 Senate districts. The only notable difference between these sessions is that Davis vetoed 608 bills and Brown vetoed 124.[14]

Examining the records of Senate and Assembly committees separately helps us determine whether term limits brought about any of the effects that we notice. We find that term limits greatly reduced experience levels in the Assembly and shortened the time horizons of Senators. By November 1996, any Assemblymember who had served continuously since 1990 had been termed out. Few of the new members who replaced them had any experience with state government, but all of them could anticipate careers in the Legislature of up to 14 years if they served the maximum term in both houses. In contrast, nearly all new Senators replacing termed-out counterparts in 1996 and 1998 had experience in the Assembly, but most of its members did not envision long legislative futures. Only a few Senators who were termed out—including Tim Leslie and Ray Haynes—moved to the Assembly.

---

[14]Our party control data are taken from tables provided electronically by the National Conference of State Legislature and our veto data are from Detwiler (2003).

For each of the four committees in each house, we tracked the histories of 30 Assembly bills assigned to the committee and 30 Senate bills.[15] Over four sessions, our sample includes data on 1,888 randomly selected pieces of legislation.[16] Here, we aggregate the actions of all of the committees in a given house; below, we look at individual committees. We also simplify our presentation by combining findings from the two pre-term limits sessions with those from the two post-term limits sessions. We do so because levels of gatekeeping and amendment activity are quite similar in the 1979–1980 and 1987–1988 sessions but shift in nearly identical ways from these years to the post-Proposition 140 sessions with which they are matched. Comparing separate descriptions of each pair demonstrates this pattern (Enemark and Cross, 2002; Abrams, 2003; Wong, 2003). Because the actions of California committees appear to fall into pre-term limits and post-term limits patterns, this is how we present the data.

Table 3.1 demonstrates how often a committee's members exercise their gatekeeping powers. It combines Assembly and Senate data for each era—the 1979–1980 and 1987–1988 sessions before Proposition 140 passed, and the 1997–1998 and 1999–2000 sessions afterward—and includes bills heard in their house of origin as well as those that have made it to the second house. Committees killed 23.8 percent of the bills assigned to them in our pre-term limits sample but only 16.5 percent after Proposition 140 took effect. This change is statistically significant at the 95 percent confidence level.[17] In both eras, most of these failing bills died a silent death when supportive committee members,

---

[15]We took these histories from the appropriate editions of the *Assembly Final History* and *Senate Final History*, published by the California Legislature. These histories have been constructed from a uniform set of forms that committee staff fill out reporting the actions taken by committees, giving us confidence that figures are comparable across committees and over time.

[16]Over four sessions, four committees in two houses hearing at least 30 bills from each house might have combined to hear 1,920 bills. Our sample includes only 1,888 because some committees were assigned fewer than 30 bills from the other house in some sessions.

[17]This "confidence statement" is a statistical phrase stating that we would see a difference in means this large in only 5 percent of cases if term limits had no actual effect on the number of supplemental reports.

Table 3.1

How Often Do Committees Exercise Gatekeeping Power?

	Before Term Limits	After Term Limits
Bills assigned to committees	958	930
Bills passing committee	730	777
Bills held in committee or failed passage	213	141
Bills withdrawn by author	15	12
% of bills passing	76.2	83.5
% of bills dying	23.8	16.5

Figures based on bill histories listed in appropriate editions of the *Senate Final History* and *Assembly Final History*, collected by Dan Enemark, Drew Cross, Matt Abrams, and Christina Wong.

anticipating the preferences of their colleagues, did not ask for a vote on a bill, and a handful of bills were withdrawn by a pessimistic author.[18] Regardless of their methods, committees have exercised their gatekeeping power less frequently since term limits were implemented.

Term limits may have weakened gatekeeping because inexperienced legislators do not have the expertise to identify problematic legislation and thus kill fewer bills. An alternative explanation is that term limits make legislators more likely to defer to their colleagues even if they suspect that their bills are ill-conceived. The basis for this "deference to colleagues" explanation is the belief that term limits make legislators less responsible for the long-term consequences of bad policy and more attuned to preserving relationships in the short term.

We can test these hypotheses by comparing the actions of Assembly committees, whose members are inexperienced but have reasonably long time horizons, with Senate committees filled with veterans on their way out. If inexperience is to blame for the decline in gatekeeping, we should see the sharpest decline in the Assembly. If deference is at work, Senators with short time horizons should account for the drop. The data suggest that inexperience is the primary force behind the reduction in

[18]Assembly rules require that a committee member make a motion to pass a bill and that one other committee member second the motion. The Senate requires a single motion.

gatekeeping, with deference to colleagues driving the trend to a lesser extent.

Assembly gatekeeping decreased drastically after term limits, whereas the decline in the Senate was smaller (Table 3.2). Before term limits, Assemblymembers killed 36.3 percent of their colleagues' proposals, but this proportion fell to 23.3 percent after Proposition 140. This decline could be driven either by deference to colleagues or by inexperience because it shows how the newest members treated the legislation of their closest colleagues. Trends in the Senate suggest that inexperience is also the primary factor driving the decline in gatekeeping. The overall decline in gatekeeping is smaller for the veteran upper house (6.2 percentage points) than it is in the Assembly (8.4 percentage points), and Senators today are nearly as tough on their colleagues' bills as they were before term limits (a 5.6 point drop that is not statistically significant), suggesting that they are not placating their colleagues. In fact, the most dramatic drop in gatekeeping by Senate committees comes in their consideration of Assembly bills (a 6.7 point, statistically significant

Table 3.2

Gatekeeping in California's Policy Committees

		% of Bills That Fail in Committee	
When Committees from This House...	Hear Bills from This House...	Before Term Limits	After Term Limits
Assembly	Assembly bills	**36.3**	**23.3**
	Senate bills	16.8	12.4
Senate	Senate bills	28.9	23.3
	Assembly bills	**13.0**	**6.3**
Overall	House of Origin bills	**32.6**	**23.3**
	Other House bills	**14.9**	**9.1**
	Assembly Committees	**26.6**	**18.2**
	Senate Committees	**21.0**	**14.8**
	Total	**23.8**	**16.5**

Figures based on bill histories listed in appropriate editions of the *Senate Final History* and *Assembly Final History*, collected by Dan Enemark, Drew Cross, Matt Abrams, and Christina Wong. Boldface indicates that the proportion of bills reported before term limits in any category differs from the proportion reported after term limits, at the 95 percent confidence level in a two-tailed test of significance.

decline), which were not screened thoroughly in their house of origin. The overall lesson, however, is the nearly universal drop in gatekeeping in both houses.[19]

Another major duty of committees is to shape the bills that they pass through the amendment process. We cannot systematically determine whether term limits have made amendments in committee more or less sophisticated, but using bill histories, we can record how often amendments have been made. We find that the rate at which committees have amended the bills that they pass has remained fairly constant (Table 3.3).[20] On average, committees amended 46.3 percent of bills in the two sessions held before 1990 and 49.4 percent of bills in the two sessions held afterward, a difference that is not statistically significant. Although we cannot tell how many amendments were made to each bill in its policy committee hearing or how long or thoughtful these amendments were, our imperfect measure shows us that committees have consistently altered about half of the bills that they pass.

Table 3.3 also suggests that after post–term limits committees were finished with bills, much work remained to be done on them. This work could involve redrafting a bill to make it accomplish all of its author's goals or to satisfy the requests of lobbyists. The portion of bills amended in other committees (in most cases, the Appropriations Committee) increased by 7.3 percentage points overall, with the largest increase coming after bills were heard in Senate policy committees. The percentage of bills amended on the floor of each house increased by about 5 percentage points, a rise that consistently registered as statistically significant.[21] Senators now rewrite a much larger percentage

[19]There has not been a similarly large increase in the percentage of introduced bills that have become law. So where does gatekeeping take place? Our data collection shows that policy committees have been replaced in their gatekeeping function to some extent by appropriations committees and to a larger extent by governors wielding their veto pens.

[20]Each category in the table examines bills that *succeed* at a given stage in the legislative process. For instance, the third row reports the percentages of bills that *pass* on the floor of their house of origin and then are amended.

[21]Most floor amendments in the California Legislature are made by bill authors themselves (often working with interest groups) rather than by the opponents of

Table 3.3

Percentage of Bills Amended at Least Once at Various Stages of the Legislative Process

	Bills Heard by Assembly Committees		Bills Heard by Senate Committees		Overall	
Origin of Amendment	Before Prop. 140	After Prop. 140	Before Prop. 140	After Prop. 140	Before Prop. 140	After Prop. 140
In policy committee	49.3	50.0	43.5	48.9	46.3	49.4
In another committee	27.4	30.4	**19.4**	**30.6**	**23.2**	**30.5**
On the floor	**36.6**	**41.7**	**32.7**	**39.8**	**34.6**	**40.7**
In the second house	**71.8**	**87.8**	79.0	74.6	75.7	81.7
Amended by author	**43.5**	**55.3**	**47.5**	**58.3**	**45.5**	**56.9**
Average Number of Amendments Made to Bills at Stages						
In the second house	**1.84**	**2.28**	2.14	2.02	2.00	2.16
Amended by author	**0.64**	**0.79**	**0.75**	**0.93**	**0.70**	**0.86**
Total amendments	**3.82**	**4.48**	**3.66**	**4.28**	**3.74**	**4.38**

Figures based on bill histories listed in appropriate editions of the *Senate Final History* and *Assembly Final History*, collected by Dan Enemark, Drew Cross, Matt Abrams, and Christina Wong. Boldface indicates that the proportion of bills reported before term limits in any category differs from the proportion reported after term limits, at the 95 percent confidence level in a two-tailed test of significance.

of Assembly bills, although the percentage of Senate bills amended in the Assembly actually dropped over the period of our study. Since term limits were imposed, bill authors, who are allowed to unilaterally amend their bills at any point in the process, have also changed a larger proportion of their own bills. Because bills can be amended at different stages of the process by authors and in the second house in which they are heard, we can count the number of times that they are amended in these ways. Again, we find that authors altered their bills more often after Proposition 140 and that Assembly bills were more frequently rewritten in the Senate.

All told, these findings point to a subtle decline in the committee amendment process. Admittedly, committees still amend about half

legislation. Still, the increase in floor amendments demonstrates that pieces of legislation emerge from policy committees unfinished.

the bills that they pass, and these amendments may be as sophisticated as they always were. However, the fact that amendments are now made more frequently at nearly every subsequent stage of the legislative process indicates that bills passed out of committees need more "fixing" or that less deference is given to committees. Either way, the patterns support the contention that term limits have eroded the committee process.

Linking Committee Experience to Committee Behavior

Differences in Senate and Assembly committee behavior are consistent with the hypothesis that the drop in experience of committee chairs has driven the reduction in gatekeeping and changes in amendment patterns. To further confirm this conclusion, we investigate the link between experience and behavior in specific committees. In each of our post-term limits sessions, we identify the committee with the least experienced chair. We then track the committee's behavior, and compare it to the same committee in a comparable session held before the passage of Proposition 140.

Sacramento Bee columnist Dan Walters explains that, since term limits, "Freshman Democrats show up in December and they say, 'Here's your office. The bathroom's down the hall. And by the way, you're a committee chairman'" (Walters, 2001). Assemblyman Darrell Steinberg, for example, was first elected in November 1998 and was appointed chair of the Assembly Labor and Employment Committee. How did he fare compared to his pre-term limits counterpart? Our sample of bills from the 1999–2000 session includes 50 bills that were assigned to Steinberg's committee. Forty-three passed, giving the committee a gatekeeping rate of 14 percent. The Labor Committee amended only 13 of these bills, but as the 43 passed bills worked their way through the legislative process, they were collectively amended 14 times by other Assembly committees and a dozen times on the Assembly floor. The 14 Assembly bills that advanced to the Senate were altered 25 times in that body. The frequency of amendments at other points in the process suggests that these bills were not finished products when they emerged from Steinberg's committee.

Contrast these figures to the record of the Labor Committee during the 1979–1980 session, when it was chaired by Bill Lockyer. Although Lockyer was in his first term as chair and had no prior experience on the committee, he had served in the Assembly since 1972. His committee approved only 46 of the 60 bills assigned to it, a gatekeeping rate of 23.3 percent, and amended 20 of these bills. After passing out of the Labor Committee, these 46 bills were amended nine times in other committees and four times on the floor. In the Senate, 19 amendments were made to the 18 Assembly bills that had been moved out of Lockyer's committee. The deference shown to the committee's work indicates that it did a better job of screening and shaping labor legislation before term limits than afterward.

Although none of the four committees we looked at had a first-year chair in the 1997–1998 session, the Assembly Judiciary Committee was led by Martha Escutia, who had not served on the committee in her first two terms. Her committee passed 51 of the 60 sampled bills assigned to it, for a gatekeeping rate of 15 percent, and amended 24 of them. All told, these 51 bills were amended nine times in other committees and 45 times on the Assembly floor. The 18 bills that progressed to the Senate were amended 54 times there.

This record differs sharply from that of the Assembly Judiciary Committee under Jack Fenton, who in 1979–1980 was in his second term as chair and serving his eighth term in the Assembly. In that session, Assembly Judiciary passed 38 of the 59 sampled bills assigned to it, a 35.6 percent gatekeeping record. The committee amended 22 of these bills, which were altered only four times in other committees and 30 times on the floor. A total of 14 bills passed by the body went on to the Senate, where they were altered 25 times. In short, the Assembly Judiciary Committee performed more than twice as much gatekeeping under Fenton as it did under Escutia, and its bills were amended about half as often at later stages of the process. These comparisons also indicate that the abrupt losses in the experience levels of committees brought by term limits have contributed to the weakening of the committee process.

Changes in Overall Staff and Floor Process

Reduction in the Expert Staff

> Prop. 140 killed the staff, because Jesse Unruh had brought the best and brightest into places like the Assembly Office of Research, which is now defunct. They wrote the last big round of important legislation in California.
>
> — former Assembly committee chair.[22]

> [When Prop. 140 mandated staff cuts,] the Assembly took that right out of their policy staff, and fired the experienced, expensive people, hired more, very inexperienced, very inexpensive staffers, and mostly campaign people. In the Senate, the old-time staffers, who have been around a while and understood the nuances, remained. And the difference is like night and day for us.
>
> — lobbyist Ken Emanuels (2001).

At the same time that it imposed term limits, Proposition 140 mandated dramatic cuts in Sacramento's legislative expenditures. In their ballot argument for Proposition 140, supporters proclaimed that the cuts would remove "political staffers" and reduce "patronage." We examined staff records to determine whether these were the sorts of staff positions that were eliminated by the term limits proposition. We found that instead of cutting the size of personal staffs, which often provide partisan political advice for members, the Legislature subverted the will of Proposition 140's backers by eliminating many nonpartisan aides. Along with many voluntary retirements, this outcome led to an immense loss in policy expertise.

Immediately after Proposition 140's passage, spending limits forced the Legislature to trim its annual budget from $214 million to $167.5 million, a 22 percent drop. However, staff levels declined only 12.5 percent between 1988 and 1996, in part because many of the most senior (and thus highest paid) staff members left during this period.[23]

[22] Interview by Karl Kurtz and Thad Kousser, Sacramento, California, February 28, 2002.

[23] Legislative budget and staff figures were obtained from the National Conference of State Legislatures.

The Legislature also shifted its staff cuts from personal staff to three units that employed more senior policy experts. Figure 3.5 tracks staffing levels at the Legislative Analyst's Office (LAO), the Senate Office of Research (SOR), and the (now defunct) Assembly Office of Research (AOR).

Each organization lost between 33 percent and 100 percent of its full-time equivalent positions, with the sharpest drop coming immediately in the wake of Proposition 140. The groups have been forced to discontinue some of their functions, such as the Legislative Analyst's analysis of the fiscal effect of bills before they are heard in Appropriations Committees. We could not obtain data to investigate this pattern, but many capitol observers have noted that it has been repeated within the ranks of personal staff. Veteran staffers with much expertise but high salaries have been phased out in favor of younger, cheaper staff who have often proven themselves to new members through their service in campaigns. The structure of the staffing cuts brought by Proposition 140—which hit policy experts especially hard—does not seem to match the intentions of the initiative's backers or appear to represent a wise allocation of resources.

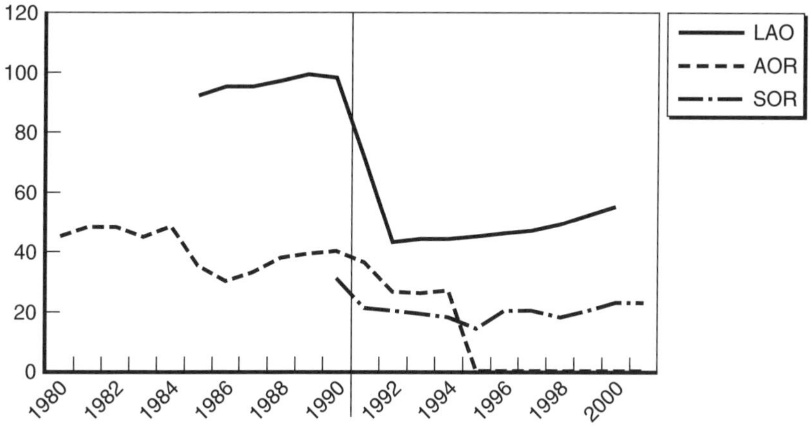

Data collected from each staffing organization by Kelly Yang.

Figure 3.5—Decline in Expert Legislative Staff After Proposition 140

Shifts in the Practice of Floor Process

> Nearly 400 bills have been amended in the past week, including dozens that have been "gutted and amended," meaning the entire contents of one measure have been deleted and replaced with a new proposal.
>
> — *Sacramento Bee* reporter Jim Sanders, September 11, 2003.

> The California Legislature has an unfortunate habit of writing legislation with multibillion-dollar consequences in the final hours of its annual session, unfortunate because these sweeping decrees often backfire. . . . Dozens of "gut and amend" measures are surfacing this week.
>
> — *Sacramento Bee* columnist Dan Walters, September 10, 2003.

Unlike many other legislatures, California's has made no formal changes in its legislative process to adapt to the effects of term limits.[24] This does not mean, however, that the practice of making laws has remained the same. One noticeable feature of California's legislative process today is the quick consideration of bills that have been gutted of their original contents and amended with entirely new content. This maneuver, which we refer to as the "hijacking" of legislation when executed by someone other than the bill's original author, has become a standard feature of the final days (and nights) of a legislative session. Although both houses took steps in 1982 to make this maneuver more difficult, it is still practiced quite often.[25] In this section, we explore whether hijacking has taken place more frequently since the implementation of term limits.

Research assistant Drew Cross devised the method for identifying hijacked bills from the thousands of pieces of legislation introduced each session in California. Cross began by eliminating from consideration the bills that failed in their house of origin because a

---

[24]For a compilation of process changes in the first 11 states to implement term limits, see Kousser (2002b).

[25]According to interviews with parliamentary staff, the 1982 changes instituted by Willie Brown and David Roberti guaranteed the right of a committee to rehear any bill that had failed on a recorded committee vote and then been "substantially amended." The changes also made it more likely that the germaneness of a significant amendment would be challenged. However, both of these rules can be suspended by a simple majority vote, as they often are.

candidate for hijacking must have already approached the end of the legislative process. He then read the subject line of every version of every bill that passed from one house to another. If, in any of the amended versions, the subject line on the bill completely changed the section of code it affected, he flagged the bill. This sort of change indicates that the content of the bill was altered radically. After flagging potential hijackings, Cross examined the text of the bills to determine whether the vast majority of the language had been changed. When a bill's language had been completely changed—indicated by italicized new text and stricken out old text with no carryover from the previous draft—he classified it as a hijacked bill.

Table 3.4 reports the frequency of hijacking in the 1993–1994 and the 1997–1998 sessions. Because Cross's method requires access to every draft of every bill in a legislative session, it was impractical for sessions in which legislative records are not available electronically. Because the Legislature's online legislative information service provides records that date back to the 1993–1994 session, this is where we began. Proposition 140 had already passed by this time but was still two years from removing the first large group of members from the Legislature. Democrats controlled both houses in 1993–1994 just as they did in 1997–1998, and Pete Wilson was governor during both sessions. Although we would rather have information on a session held before the

Table 3.4

The Frequency of Bill Hijackings

	1993–1994		1997–1998	
	Senate Bills	Assembly Bills	Senate Bills	Assembly Bills
Total number of bills introduced	2138	3838	2242	2817
Number passed to second house	1422	2395	741	1813
Hijacked bills	56	119	51	162
% of introduced bills that are hijacked	2.6	3.1	2.3	5.8

Data collected from legislative records websites linked to www.sen.ca.gov and www.assembly.ca.gov and analyzed by Drew Cross.

passage of Proposition 140, these sessions still provide information about the effect of term limits on hijacking.

In both sessions, the hijacking of Assembly bills, which takes place in the Senate, was much more frequent than the hijacking of Senate bills. Term limits have had little effect on the rate of hijacking performed in the lower house, but they appear to have led to takeovers of many more Assembly bills by members of the upper house. Overall, this trend increased the total number of hijackings from 175 bills during the 1993–1994 session to 213 in 1997–1998. Because the number of Assembly bills introduced declined by over 1,000 pieces of legislation, the rate at which they are hijacked in the last stages of the legislative process has nearly doubled.

How likely are hijacked bills to pass? Because they usually represent late-session deals, and because their substantive contents avoid many obstacles in the legislative process, their passage would seem to be a fait accompli. Yet during the 1993–1994 session, only 57 of the 119 Assembly bills that were hijacked and 34 of the 56 similar Senate bills ultimately passed, a success rate of 52 percent. This hardly improved in 1997–1998, when 87 of the 162 hijacked Assembly bills and 29 of the 51 Senate bills that had been taken over passed, a rate of 54.4 percent. Although hijacking may be more commonplace after term limits, passage of the final bill is hardly assured.

Does the increase in bill hijacking mean that California's legislative process has been gravely injured? When completely new subject matter is allowed to bypass gatekeeping and amending in committees, the level of policy scrutiny declines.[26] Coming late in the session, hijacked bills also receive less comment from interest groups and the general public than bills that work their way through the Legislature on the usual time schedule. This is another definite harm.

Yet some reasonable justifications have been offered for inserting new content into a bill in the last stages of the process. According to one

---

[26]Even when a committee is allowed to hear a bill "off the floor" in the closing days of the legislative session, the legislation receives less analysis and review than it would in a regularly scheduled hearing.

legislative staffer, hijacking can be used to prevent spending bills from amendments that give every legislator a bit of pork.[27] When a spending bill works its way through the process, legislators in many committees may ask for money for their districts. This is reportedly what happened with Assembly Bill 12, which became the parks bond (Proposition 12) on the March 2000 ballot. The environmental leaders in the Legislature learned their lesson, and when they prepared the legislation that would become Proposition 40 on the March, 2002 ballot, they hijacked a bill (Assembly Bill 1602) late in the process so that fewer legislators were able to extract pork from it. Legislators also use late-session amendments to avoid minority party obstruction when an author who had missed a bill deadline would otherwise have been required to get a waiver by a unanimous or a supermajority vote. Perhaps most frequently, however, hijackings are used to implement a late deal completed by legislative leaders, who may argue that important compromises most often come toward the end of session, and some means of fast-tracking these deals is a necessary legislative evil.

Realizing that there has been an increase in hijackings during the post-term limits era, some leaders have sought to change the way that bills are treated at the end of the session. One Assembly Speaker slowed down the process at the end of a session to give more scrutiny to hijacked bills. Some bills died as time ran out, but the Speaker defends his decision. "The media's take on the disorganization in the final days of the 2000 session was inaccurate, but I didn't fight the spin," he said. "The Senate sent me 128 bills that had been cut-and-pasted with new content, and I decided to give them hearings." To prevent another end-of-session crunch, the Speaker brought together the authors of overlapping bills at the start of the next session and thereby helped to remove 140 bills from the Assembly's workload.[28]

---

[27]Telephone interview by Thad Kousser, March 18, 2002.

[28]Interview by Karl Kurtz and Thad Kousser, Sacramento, California, February 25, 2002.

The Content of Policy

> It is a myth that you can't make deals anymore. The Legislature has come together on many important compromises, like the $9.2 billion school bond that also changed developer fees, a longstanding, unresolved issue.
>
> — Former Assemblymember.[29]

> Long-term issues get ignored, and legislation is smaller and crappier. I'm not sure that they are capable of dealing with large policy issues like water and growth. Some of that is realizing that they won't get these through the governor, and they don't bother trying. Under term limits, you get people wanting to have something to put on their campaign brochure so that they can run for the next office.
>
> — Senate committee consultant.[30]

> There is absolutely less interest in the long-term, non-sexy issues. You don't have members pushing legislation that will show its fruits ten years from now; it is of little value to them.
>
> — Senate committee consultant.[31]

Perhaps the most important question we can ask is whether term limits have affected the quality of bills produced by the California Legislature. However, it is also the most difficult question we seek to answer. Gauging the quality of a piece of legislation is fraught with normative, partisan, and practical difficulties. Although many thinkers have advanced coherent rules for achieving "the good" in social decisions, there is no consensus among political theorists about what constitutes good government. California's major parties have obvious differences about what constitutes quality legislation or even the desirability of new

---

[29]Interview by Karl Kurtz and Thad Kousser, Sacramento, California, February 25, 2002.

[30]Telephone interview by Thad Kousser, July 25, 2001.

[31]Telephone interview by Thad Kousser, August 2001.

laws at all.[32] Finally, comparing bills across eras can be tricky when our only information about a pre-1990s bill is the text itself.

Rather than attempting to make broad subjective judgments about the quality of legislation, we borrow two (admittedly flawed) measures of legislative content from state policy analysts and from work in comparative politics. The first estimates the "breadth" of a bill by counting the number of California Government Code chapters and sections that it alters. The second calculates "complexity" with a standardized accounting of the length of bills in their final form. We use both to judge Proposition 140's effect on bills that became law.

Our claim here is modest. Lacking a clear consensus on whether legislation is good or bad in most instances, we ask a more limited question: Is the legislation today, as some suggested to us in interviews, narrower in scope and complexity? Do term-limited members fall back on smaller and less ambitious legislation because they lack the time or expertise to develop broader, more complex bills? The reasons to think so lie in the evidence we have already presented demonstrating declines in experience levels and committee expertise. Alternatively, the scope of legislation may have remained the same. This may be the case because post-term limits legislators have received substantial assistance from lobbyists and nonpartisan staff in drafting bills or because the Senate has compensated for the Assembly's lack of experience and expertise.

Our measure of the breadth of legislation is inspired by a historical analysis of natural resources laws passed by Maine's Legislature. Pat Norton of the Maine's Office of Policy and Legal Analysis compared bills over many sessions by counting how many chapters and sections of Maine law they affected. The shifts in legislative breadth that he documented in this fashion matched his subjective observations. In our California analysis, we first count the number of California Codes—such as the Welfare and Institutions Code, the Labor Code, or the Penal Code—that a bill affects. Then we record separate measures of how many sections (subparts of the chapters) the legislation adds, deletes, or

[32]The legislative director of a conservative Republican Senator told us that when the Senator was first elected, he did not want to introduce any bills at all. He eventually relented on the condition that all of his bills would seek to repeal existing laws.

amends. The purpose of this approach is to capture the concept of breadth in two of its possible meanings. A bill is broad in its subject matter if it alters many chapters of a state's code. The effect of a bill is broad if it alters many sections of these chapters. Legislation that changes many sections across multiple chapters is the broadest of all.

To gauge the complexity of bills, we rely on the simple statistic of the bill's length at the time of final passage. This is the same measure used by Huber and Shipan (2002) to compare legislation produced by industrialized democracies. Complexity may not be a universally desired characteristic of legislation, but it is likely to be highly correlated with bill length. To make comparisons across sessions in California, we use the Code Sections Affected for each session, recording the number of lines in each bill.

Admittedly, these measures are imperfect. The hope of social scientists is always that random sources of error—a complex bill that happens to be short, or a narrow bill that somehow affects many sections of many code chapters—are rare and will "average out" once these measures are applied to hundreds of bills. We also conducted a pilot project to test the validity of our measures. Through the Legislative Information Service website, we accessed committee analyses that provide background on bills, describe how they change existing law, and summarize the arguments for supporting or opposing them.[33] An author and research assistant independently read analyses of the final versions of 50 bills and assigned subjective breadth and complexity scores to each.[34] On our breadth scale, we categorized a bill as a district bill, an issue of small statewide concern, an issue of medium statewide concern, or an

---

[33]Unfortunately, committee analyses are not available in electronic format in any session before term limits. Furthermore, the effect of term limits on the staff who prepared the analyses might bias the use of this measure.

[34]For this pilot project, we randomly sampled 25 Assembly bills and 25 Senate bills from the list of bills that became law in the 1997-1998 session. We sampled only bills labeled as SBs and ABs and did not look at resolutions of any type. Thad Kousser and researcher Natalie Freese assigned the subjective scores, and Freese completed the quantifications. If at all possible, we did not look at the actual text of bills before assigning our scores, as this would expose the bill's length to us. In some instances, however, we felt we needed to read the bill to understand its intent fully, potentially increasing the chances that our subjective measure of complexity and our objective quantification of a bill's length would be correlated.

issue of major statewide concern. On our complexity scale, we labeled legislation as simple, fairly complex, or very complex.

The scores assigned to bills were quite similar. We put bills in exactly the same category in 53 percent of cases, and in only 2 percent of cases did our judgments differ by more than one category. For each bill, we then recorded our objective measures of breadth and complexity to see how closely they were correlated with our subjective judgments. As Figures 3.6 and 3.7 indicate, there was a tight relationship. Values of the

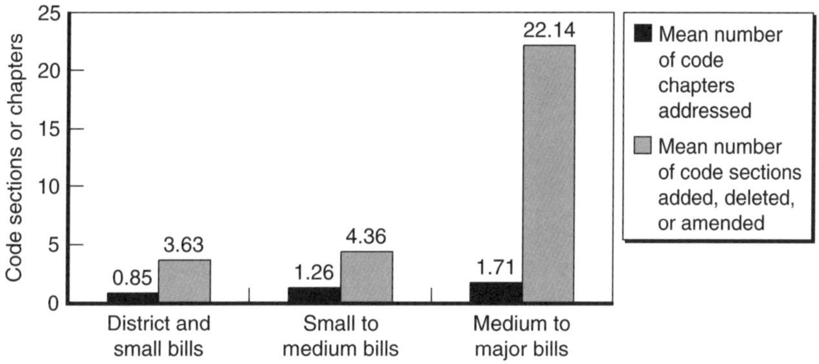

Figure 3.6—Breadth of Legislation: Subjective and Objective Measures

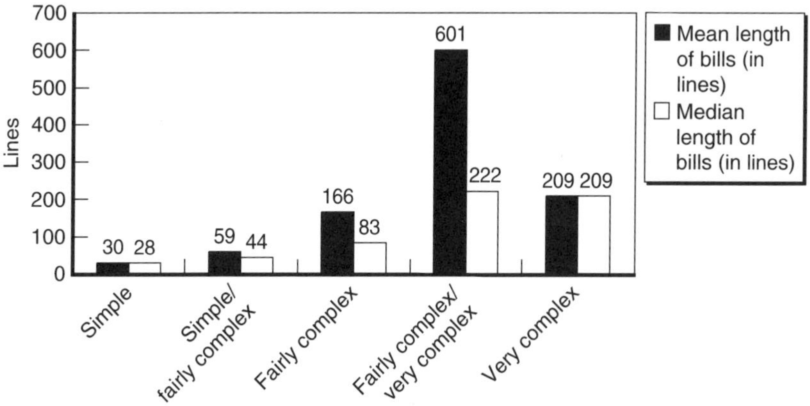

Figure 3.7—Complexity of Legislation: Subjective and Objective Measures

objective measures increase steadily for bills that we put in the higher categories of breadth and complexity. Figure 3.6 shows that the bills we labeled as broader addressed more code chapters and affected more sections within these chapters.[35] Figure 3.7 shows that the legislation that we judged to be more complex also tended to be longer (with the exception of the two bills in the "very complex" category).

Satisfied that we could reliably quantify the breadth and complexity of bills passed before and after term limits, we applied our measures to a large sample of bills from the same two pairs of sessions studied throughout this section. This sample draws between 200 and 300 bills in each session, ensuring that each bill in each session has an equal chance of being selected. Reviewing the chaptered version of each bill in a format that has remained consistent over time, our research assistants recorded how many California Codes the bill altered, how many sections within the codes it added, amended, or deleted, and how many lines long it was. We expected to find that the scope of successful legislation had become narrower after term limits and that chaptered bills were now shorter and simpler.

Data on the breadth of Senate bills tell exactly the opposite story (Figure 3.8). The average number of codes altered by SBs has grown slightly as the number of sections affected has increased. Comparing the matched pairs of sessions that hold other political factors constant—1979–1980 vs. 1999–2000 and 1987–1988 vs. 1997–1898—indicates that term limits have brought 25–50 percent increases in some of these objective measures. Surprisingly, the Senate seems to be producing more substantial legislation after term limits. Could it be that this represents a shift in the Legislature's workload to the upper house, while breadth and complexity in the Assembly has dramatically decreased?

---

[35]Five of the bills in our sample—direct appropriations and budget-related legislation—did not amend an existing code, and we therefore assigned them a value of zero in our "number of codes addressed" quantification. This meant that the bills we judged to be district bills or small issues of statewide concern addressed, on average, less than one code section.

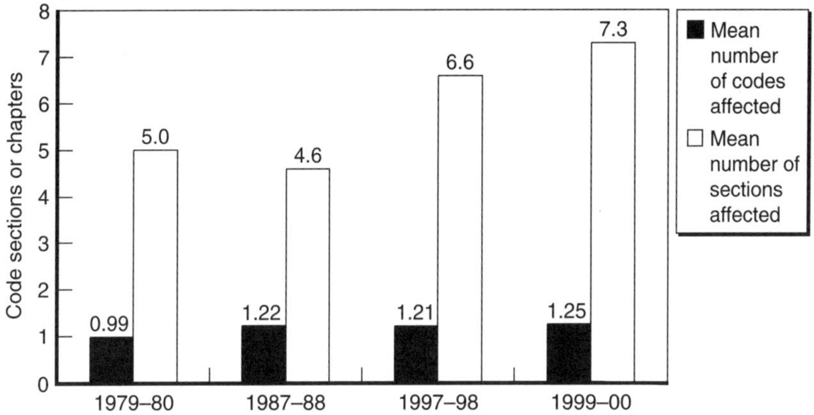

Collected from the chaptered text of 407 bills by Natalie Freese and Jessika Palmer.

Figure 3.8—Breadth of Senate Legislation Before and After Term Limits

This does not appear to be the story told by Figure 3.9, especially when we consider how one outlying bill from the 1979–1980 session contributes to an exceptional pattern in the chart. In this session, the mean number of sections affected is high in part because of one bill, Alister McAlister's AB 261, which ran 5,917 lines and changed 684

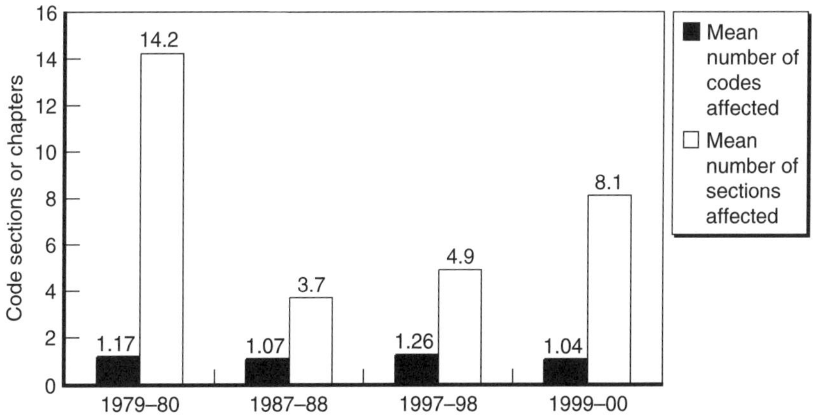

Collected from the chaptered text of 581 bills by Natalie Freese and Jessika Palmer.

Figure 3.9—Breadth of Assembly Legislation Before and After Term Limits

sections of the Probate Code. Remove this bill from the sample and the new mean is 7.1 sections affected, which is smaller than the mean of 8.1 sections affected in the comparable 1999–2000 session. Although the number of codes affected dropped slightly in the pair, both this measure and the mean number of sections affected increased from 1987–1988 to 1997–1998. In the Assembly as in the Senate, the bills that become law after term limits appear broader than previous legislation.

Finally, term limits have been associated with a surprising increase in our measure of complexity, the median number of lines per chaptered bill (Figure 3.10). Looking at both Senate and Assembly bills, comparisons of both 1979–1980 vs. 1999–2000 and 1987–1988 vs. 1997–1998 show that the length of bills has grown by between 15 percent and 90 percent.

What can be driving this trend? One Assemblymember credited with being a policy heavyweight in the post-term limits era offers an explanation. "The sense of urgency that term limits created has been both a positive and negative factor for policy," says the member. "It allows relatively new members with new energy not to have to wait their turn to make an impact. If you are focused, you can come in and get

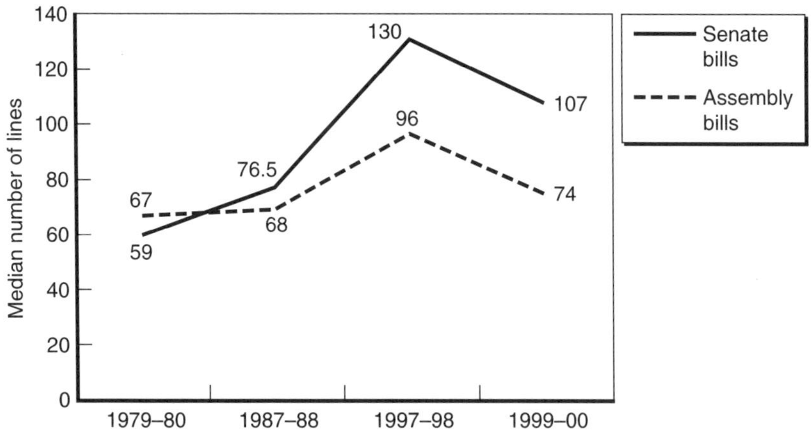

Collected from the chaptered text of 989 bills by Natalie Freese and Jessika Palmer.

Figure 3.10—Complexity of Legislation Before and After Term Limits

things done quickly. That's a positive impact on policy. For me, it's been like being a kid in a candy store." One of our reviewers offered another reasonable explanation. Term-limited legislators who know that they will not be around long enough to oversee the bureaucracy's implementation of their legislation may attempt to lock in their intentions by crafting very specific bills. Another reviewer surmised that increasingly complicated bills may be a function of an ever more complicated society and a body of existing law that grows over time. Whatever the reason for the recent increase in the breadth and complexity of legislation, it appears to us that this counterintuitive trend cannot be dismissed.

4. Party Leadership and Partisan Polarization

A primary motive behind Proposition 140, made explicit by its backers, was to rid Sacramento of the dictatorial leadership and extreme partisanship that, in their contention, characterized the 1980s. The initiative's primary booster, former Los Angeles County Supervisor Pete Schabarum, targeted what he saw as the disproportionate authority wielded by longtime Assembly Speaker Willie Brown. "As Huey Long was once the Kingfish of Louisiana politics," Schabarum wrote in his review of the campaign, "Willie Brown is today's flamboyant symbol of California Politics" (Schabarum, 1992, p. 21). Term-limit proponents also pointed to the bitter battles between the parties as an evil that could be undone by exiling those who created Sacramento's partisan culture. Critics of the initiative warned that term limits would replace these legislators with extremists with even fewer incentives to compromise.

In this chapter, we introduce methods for measuring the dominance of leaders and partisan polarization. These measures allow us to evaluate how powerful leaders were and how far apart the parties were situated before and after term limits. Although legislative leaders, especially those in the Assembly, now have much shorter reigns, we find no evidence that their position in Sacramento's power structure has weakened. Our examination of party polarization shows that term limits have not led to the election of ideologically extreme legislators. When members are about to be termed out of the Legislature, they vote with their parties more often than they otherwise might have, but term limits also stop their drift to the wings of each caucus. These effects are countervailing, but in combination they show that term limits have neither accelerated nor slowed down California's increasing party polarization. The overall lesson of this chapter is that, despite predictions that Proposition 140 would bring great change in these areas, it does not appear to have transformed the power of California's leaders or widened the gulf between its parties.

Party Leadership

Term limits have obviously shortened the reigns of party leaders, especially in the Assembly. The simple math of a six-year Assembly career means that aspiring party chiefs must impress their colleagues in their first terms, fight leadership battles in their second terms, and struggle to remain relevant in their final, lame duck terms. One veteran staffer who has worked for several Speakers reported that, "Even before a new Speaker is elected, people are jockeying for the next Speakership."[1] According to a member of the Assembly Republican leadership team, "The current freshman class is talking about who will be the leaders in 2004 and jockeying for position."[2]

In the seven years since term limits were implemented, there have been five Assembly Speakers and even more minority party leaders. Table 4.1 compares this constant churning with typical tenure lengths throughout the Legislature's "professional" era.[3] Nine Speakers have wielded the gavel since 1995; only five Speakers reigned from 1961 until 1995. A former Speaker puts these figures into historical perspective: "About 48 or 49 of the California Assembly's Speakers served for two years or less. The long-term Speakership only came about with the reigns of Unruh and Willie Brown. . . . So we should think of the post-term limits rotation of Speakers as a return to the norm."[4] Although he is correct, the trend also recalls the days when the Legislature was less able to stand up to the executive branch or control the influence of lobbyists.[5]

---

[1]Telephone interview by Thad Kousser, August 2001.

[2]Interview by Karl Kurtz, Sacramento, California, February 26, 2002.

[3]Proposition 1A in 1966 inaugurated the era of "professionalization" in Sacramento by moving the Legislature toward full-time sessions, high salaries, and large staffs.

[4]Interview by Karl Kurtz and Thad Kousser, Sacramento, California, February 25, 2002.

[5]For a history of this era of the California Legislature, see Jacobs (1995).

Table 4.1

Legislative Leaders Since 1960

Assembly Speaker	Date of Service	Senate President pro Tempore	Date of Service
Jesse M. Unruh (Dem)	1961–1968	Hugh M. Burns (Dem)	1957–1969
Robert T. Monagan (Rep)	1969–1970	Howard Way (Rep)	1969–1970
Bob Moretti (Dem)	1971–1974	Jack Schrade (Rep)	1970
Leo T. McCarthy (Dem)	1974–1980	James R. Mills (Dem)	1971–1980
Willie Brown, Jr. (Dem)	1980–1995	David Roberti (Dem)	1980–1994
Doris Allen (Rep)	6/95–9/95	William Lockyer (Dem)	1994–1998
Brian Setencich (Rep)	9/95–1/96	John Burton (Dem)	1998–present
Curt Pringle (Rep)	1/96–12/96		
Cruz Bustamante (Dem)	12/96–2/98		
Antonio Villaraigosa (Dem)	2/98–4/00		
Robert Hertzberg (Dem)	4/00–2/02		
Herb Wesson (Dem)	2/02–2/04		
Fabian Nunez (Dem)	2/04–present		

Taken from Block and Buck (1999), pp. 233 and 379, and the Assembly's website, www.assembly.ca.gov.

The Senate leadership has been more stable, leading many to note that the Senate is now truly the upper house in California politics. Capitol strategist Donna Lucas commented, "The one person who I think does know the issues, who has been there on two tours of duty is [Senate President] John Burton. He's got some of the most veteran staff working for him" (Lucas, 2001).

Perhaps to restore the balance of power, Assembly leaders have adopted two strategies to help smooth transitions: abiding by a rotation schedule and retaining the veteran leadership staff. The National Conference of State Legislature's Rich Jones has identified a regular pattern of succession in Sacramento. "You've developed a bit of a process here in California over the last several sessions," Jones reported, "where the Assembly Speaker has stepped down and elected another Assembly Speaker midway through that person's next-to-last term" (Jones, 2001). Longtime capitol observer Tim Hodson also sees staff as being key to leaders' influence and the Legislature's performance overall. "I wonder if on the top of that there's sort of super-grade mandarins," Hodson said. "I know some people in the Speaker's office who have survived [Speakers] Bustamante, Villaraigosa, and Hertzberg, and they're just there because everybody recognizes that 'We can't run the railroad without these people'" (Hodson, 2001).

That recent legislative leaders have had shorter tenures does not necessarily mean that they have been less powerful. In Florida, for instance, House Speakers rotate every two years, but the position is said to be one of the most powerful anywhere in America. Still, much of a Speaker's power rests on his or her ability to pay off debts or exact punishments in the future. As one Assemblywoman notes, Speakers "have to be around to be able to enforce."[6] To test whether leadership power has declined, we propose a way to measure the power of leaders. Contrary to what we had expected, we find no obvious shift in Sacramento's power structure related to term limits.

Our measurement strategy is based on the presumption that smart money follows the power in Sacramento. By "smart money," we mean campaign donations given by interest groups and individual

---

[6]Interview by Bruce Cain and Cathy Ellis, Sacramento, California, August 6, 2002.

contributors, who may be seeking access to or influence over legislators. Using the campaign contribution reports made available by the Fair Political Practices Commission and the Secretary of State, we tracked how much each legislator raises from these sources as a proxy for their political power. To limit our analysis to contributions given by those who potentially seek to influence policy, we eliminated donations made to a member by a legislative leader. In most cases, these transactions are made to influence elections. They are redistributions of electoral resources that usually flow from the top leaders to their most vulnerable political allies. Instead of marking a member's strength, contributions received from leaders usually signal his or her weakness. For this reason, our measure of smart money reports a legislator's contribution totals, purged of money raised from the Assembly Speaker, the Senate President pro Tempore, and Minority and Majority Leaders in both houses. It combines primary and general election contributions for those who won office in 1988 and those who won in 1998. Both elections were held before Proposition 34 limited the size of contributions in California races.

We use this proxy for legislative power to test the hypothesis that legislative leaders are less central now than in the past. Term limits may have shifted authority to committee chairs, whose influence over a policy area might increase at the expense of legislative leaders. Or Proposition 140 might have distributed power widely across the Legislature, democratizing the body by removing such leaders as the self-described "Ayatollah of the Assembly," Willie Brown (York, 1999). To test these predictions, we divided legislators from each house into four categories.

Our groupings segregate the top legislative leaders, the party leaders, committee chairs, and rank-and-file members. We define "top leaders" in the Assembly as the Speaker, Speaker pro Tempore, Majority Leader, and Minority Leader, and in the Senate as the President pro Tempore, Majority Leader, and Minority Leader. Our "party leaders" category includes the caucus chairs and the whips from each party in each house. Any committee chair qualifies for our next grouping, and we label everyone else as a "rank-and-file" legislator. For both the Assembly and the Senate, we combine smart money contribution totals to compute the total amount of money received by all the members of each group. To control for the inflation of California campaign costs in recent decades, we express the contributions that each group received as a percentage of total donations in that year.

If Proposition 140 greatly weakened the Legislature's leadership, we would expect to see a clear shift in the distribution of contribution totals from 1988 to 1998. The top leaders in each body would raise a much lower proportion of Sacramento's money than they used to, with party leaders, committee chairs, or less prominent members taking advantage of their losses. As Yang (2001) notes, there was no such pattern in the Assembly; in fact, there is remarkable stability in the spread of campaign funds (Figure 4.1). The only major change is that leaders raised an even larger percentage of total contributions—22 percent, up from 15 percent—after the implementation of term limits. This pattern contradicts the conventional wisdom that Willie Brown dominated Sacramento's money game like no one has since his departure. The top leaders in 1998 raised more than their 1988 counterparts, at the expense of the Assembly rank-and-file.

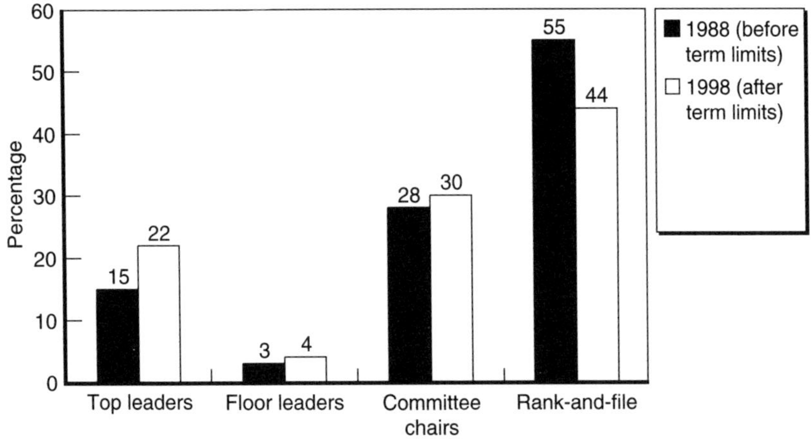

Smart money includes primary and general election contributions to each winner legislator, excluding funds transferred from the account of a top legislative leader. Data collected from Fair Political Practices Commission records by Kelly Yang.

Figure 4.1—Distribution of Smart Money Contributions in the Assembly

The pattern in the Senate is similar once we consider what is different about this dataset. Because the Senate's four-year terms are staggered, only half of the upper house's membership was up for election in 1988 or in 1998. Consequently, our proportions include only the group members who ran in each year, making the totals for small groups such as top leaders vulnerable to year-to-year fluctuations. This is a sufficient explanation for the drop in the proportion of money raised by top leaders from 1988 to 1998 (Figure 4.2). In 1988, the top leaders' category consisted only of David Roberti, the Senate's President pro Tempore and its most powerful member. The sitting President pro Tempore in 1998, Bill Lockyer, was not up for a Senate election—he was elected state attorney general that year—and the other top leaders accounted for only 5 percent of the smart money that year. However, Lockyer raised 24 percent of the contributions to Senators in the 1994 cycle, indicating that leaders are able to raise as much money after the passage of term limits as they were before.

The fact that only 20 Senators are included in each year's analysis—compared with 80 Assemblymembers—also helps explains the division

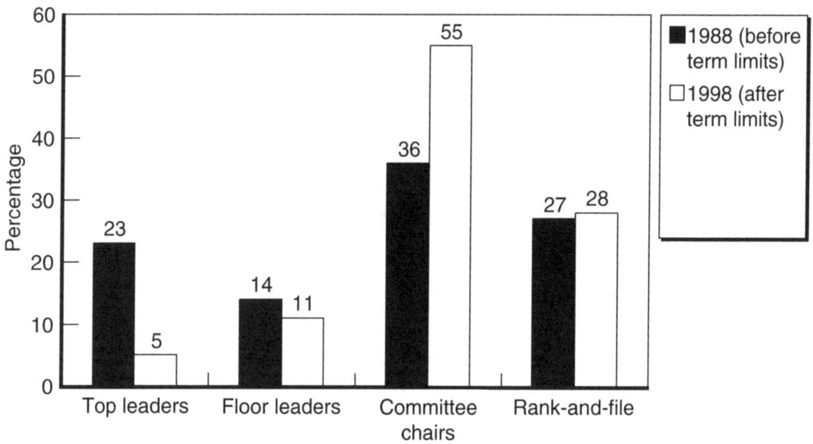

Smart money includes primary and general election contributions to each winner legislator, excluding funds transferred from the account of a top legislative leader. Data collected from Fair Political Practices Commission records by Kelly Yang.

Figure 4.2—Distribution of Smart Money Contributions in the Senate

of smart money between the Assembly and Senate in 1988 and 1998 (Figure 4.3). In each era, the Assembly raised more smart money than the Senate, presumably because each Assembly seat could be contested. The more informative pattern in the figure is the consistent division of money between the two chambers. We expected the Senate's share of smart money to grow, signaling its growing influence as the dominant house. Instead, the distribution of donations remained fairly constant from 1988 to 1998. Senators raised 27.5 percent of the money in 1988 and 24.4 percent in 1998. This surprising finding makes us skeptical

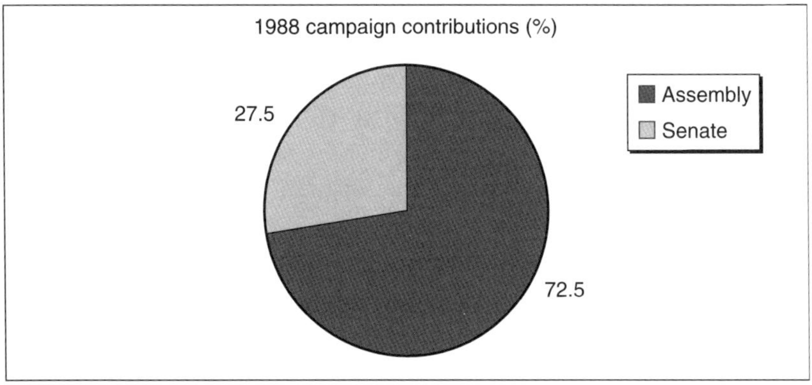

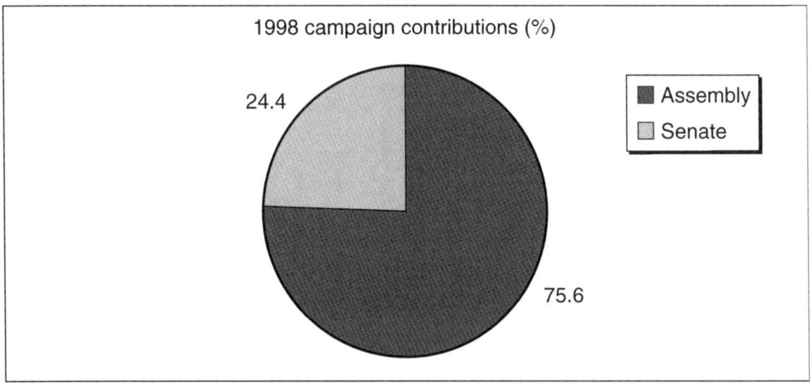

Smart Money includes primary and general election contributions to each winner legislator, excluding funds transferred from the account of a top legislative leader. Data collected from Fair Political Practices Commission records by Kelly Yang.

Figure 4.3—Division of Smart Money Contributions Between the Houses

of claims that power radically shifted toward the Senate, at least in the first session held after the implementation of Proposition 140.

What is the overall lesson of our investigation of smart money? Relative to other legislative players, leaders in the post-term limits era are as central to the fundraising process as they were before. However, many of those we interviewed doubt that today's leaders are as powerful as their pre-1990 counterparts, and our figures say nothing about the balance of power between today's legislative leaders and those outside the Legislature. Although these leaders still raise the lion's share of money in legislative elections, term limits may have increased the influence of governors, agency officials, and interest groups at their expense.

Partisan Polarization

> The single biggest effect of term limits is increased partisanship. You don't know your colleagues well, and you don't treat them as part of your future.
>
> — Former Senate committee chair.[7]

> The age of partisanship, which perhaps never had a beginning and may never have an end, at least changed by 1990, as the voters imposed term limits.
>
> — Former Senate Appropriations Chair Patrick Johnston (2001).

Recent academic studies of voting behavior in the California Legislature have verified what Sacramento inside observers long suspected: that California Republicans and Democrats are growing further apart. The two party caucuses have become tightly clustered voting blocs, and the ideological distance between these blocs has grown steadily.

To chart these changes, political scientists have used a measure of voting behavior compiled by an interest group, the AFL-CIO. Since 1911, the California State Federation of Labor, the California chapter of the AFL-CIO, has rated legislators based on a set of votes on 20 to 40 pieces of key legislation. The AFL-CIO reports both committee and

[7]Interview by Karl Kurtz and Thad Kousser, Sacramento, California, February 25, 2002.

floor votes, and since 1996, it has reported average scores for legislators over their careers. We analyzed scores based on floor votes during a given year. Although these records focus on labor issues, the scores generally reflect ideology and correlate quite closely with ratings given by organizations representing environmental, abortion rights, business, and education causes.

As Masket (2004) points out, the two-party caucuses in Sacramento have grown further apart over time. To illustrate this point, he tracks the AFL-CIO score of the median member of each party in the Assembly (Figure 4.4). The gap in raw AFL-CIO scores between the parties averaged 79.8 percentage points in the decade leading up to the passage of Proposition 140 but grew to 88.9 points in the 1990s. Using similar voting records, Jacobson (forthcoming) shows that the partisan polarization of California's Legislature mirrors trends among California's voters, political activists, and members of Congress since 1970. He notes that although the House members from the two parties once overlapped in their ideologies, the gap between California's Democrats and Republicans in Congress "grew steeply during the late 1970s and early 1980 and has since remained wide."

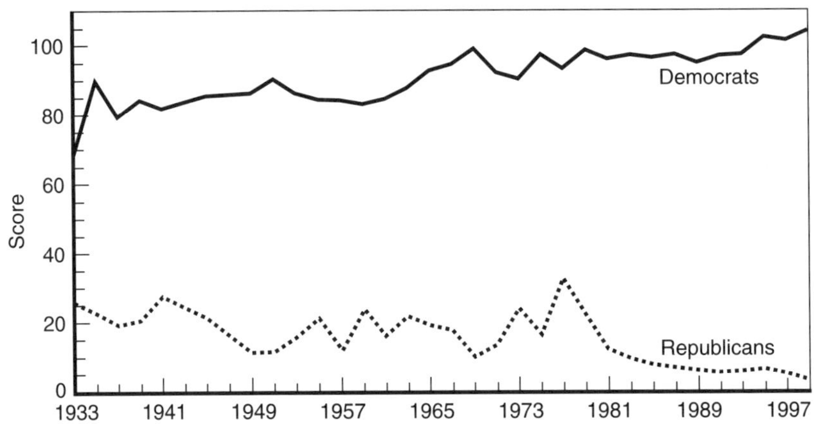

Labor scores are derived from the annual publication of the California Federation of Labor, AFL-CIO, recorded and presented by Seth Masket. Scores have been adjusted by the process described by Groseclose, Levitt, and Snyder (1999).

Figure 4.4—California Federation of Labor Scores in the Assembly for the Median Member of Each Party, 1933–1999

It seems that partisan polarization has increased over time in California and that this divergence has accelerated over the past decade. Is this trend, which coincides with the advent of term limits, caused by term limits? Other changes taking place in Sacramento during the same period might be responsible. Increased polarization in roll call voting could be the result of growing partisanship in the electorate (Jacobson, forthcoming), redistricting plans that made incumbents much safer after the 1980 and 2000 censuses (Kousser, 1997; Finnegan, 2004), contribution reporting laws that made it more costly for legislators to socialize across party lines (Enemark, 2001), or some other cause. It is impossible to rule out these alternative explanations if we examine only aggregate trends in one state. Rather than turning to other states and attempting to make imperfect comparisons, we analyze trends in the behavior of individual legislators to assess whether term limits have polarized the body as a whole. If Proposition 140 has pulled the parties apart overall, this must have occurred through a shift in each legislator's voting pattern that can be plausibly linked to term limits.

We identify three ways that term limits might influence individual legislators in a way that could increase the aggregate level of partisan polarization. Our first possible explanation assumes that members have always entered the Legislature with highly partisan views but that they drift toward the center over their careers as they moderate their views and learn the value of compromise. By expelling members just as they become more centrist, term limits ensure that a house will be composed only of newer, more partisan legislators. A second explanation posits that since the passage of Proposition 140, short terms of service in the Legislature have been attractive mostly to ideologues. This implies that they are much more partisan in their first terms than were their predecessors, who were primarily political careerists. Finally, a third potential explanation holds that new members today behave just like new members in previous decades did but that they react to the way term limits dramatically cut their time horizons. Without long-run incentives to cooperate with members of the other party, they generally stick with their caucuses in their first terms and over their brief careers.[8]

We explore these explanations using AFL-CIO scores to compare the voting careers of a "class" of legislators, first elected in 1986, with a post-limits group, the class 1996. We chose the class of 1996 because its members have now had up to three sessions to alter their behavior and the class of 1986 because it entered pre-term limits Sacramento under relatively similar political conditions.[9]

Each explanation of partisanship, if correct, would create a distinct empirical pattern in the behavior of classes. Suppose our first explanation is correct—that term limits cut off a natural drift toward center over each legislator's career. If so, members of both classes would compile more extreme first-term voting records than we might expect given the makeup of their districts. In subsequent terms, their voting records would tend to drift toward the center. In contrast, the second explanation implies that first-term voting scores for the class of 1996 would tend toward the edges of the ideological spectrum much more than the initial records of the pre-term limits class. Finally, our third explanation predicts that individual voting patterns should be static after the passage of Proposition 140. There should be no observable drift toward the center for the class of 1996 or for members of the class of 1986 once the initiative passed in November 1990.

We begin by comparing the ideological extremity of new members during their first year of voting to the records of veteran legislators. The simplest way to do this—comparing the AFL-CIO scores of new and old members—is problematic. Legislators face very different pressures from

---

[8]Still other alternatives are possible. For example, one Assemblywoman told us, "Term limits have created a rightward drift. No one votes for anything 'on the way out;' they are still careerists, but now they are thinking three jobs ahead." Interviewed by Bruce Cain and Cathy Ellis, Sacramento, California, August 6, 2002.

[9]Both the 1987–1988 and the 1997–1998 sessions were characterized by divided government, with Republican governors and Democratic-controlled Legislatures. We could find no parallel for one notable political condition that greeted the class of 1996: the extreme partisan rancor that had occurred throughout the 1995–1996 session, when Willie Brown clung to power by forming alliances with a succession of three Republican Speakers elected with only Democratic support. This could have created more partisan polarization than there otherwise might have been in the class of 1996's first session.

their constituents. A Democrat from a competitive suburban district who votes with union interests 90 percent of the time seems to us to be more of a polarized partisan than a Democrat from a safe, urban seat with the same AFL-CIO score. It is especially important to consider district pressures when examining the effects of term limits because Proposition 140 changed the nature of new members. Many of the dozen members of the Assembly's class of 1986 represented highly competitive districts because these were the types of seats that often turned over before term limits. The districts inhabited by the 32 newcomers in 1996 were a microcosm of the entire Assembly because Proposition 140's effect was blind to the safety of seats.

Consequently, to make our pre- and post-term limits analyses comparable, we present data on both district partisanship and voting behavior. Effectively, we define ideological extremists as those with highly partisan voting records relative to the partisan homogeneity of their district. Figure 4.5 displays the relationship between Democratic registration and support for union legislation for both the class of 1996 and for veteran members in the Assembly. Because only two Senators

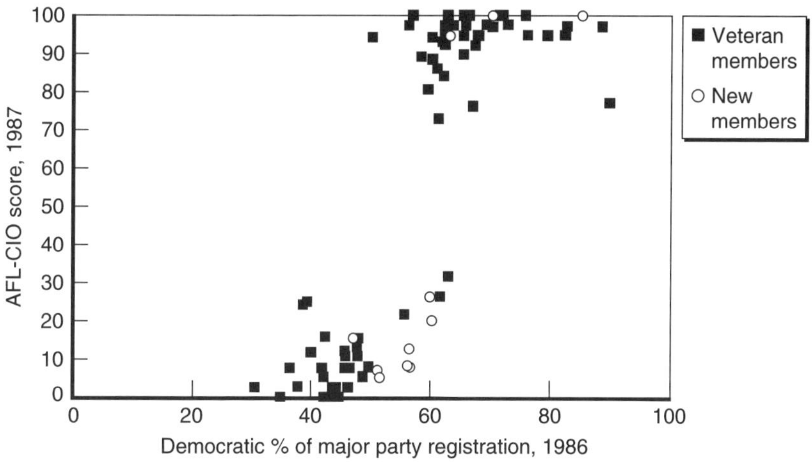

Data collected from the AFL-CIO's legislative reports and the California Secretary of State's "Statement of Registration," October 1986, by Joseph Kim and Matt Tokeshi.

Figure 4.5—Ideological Extremism in the Assembly Class of 1986

were newly elected in 1986, we do not display a scatterplot for this class. In the Assembly, the parties are clearly polarized. The voting records of their members are concentrated at the ends of the spectrum, with no Democrat voting with the AFL-CIO less than 73 percent of the time and no Republican supporting the union on more than 32 percent of votes. District registration seems to explain much of the variation within each party: The higher the Democratic registration in a district, the more likely it is that its representative supports the AFL-CIO.

We separate new members from veterans to examine this key relationship. If the class of 1986 were just as ideologically extreme as the experienced members, the circles representing them would be lost in a sea of squares depicting other members. Instead, the new Republicans (nine of the 12 new members) stand out from the veteran legislators in their caucus. Located to the right of most other Republicans, these members have more conservative voting records than we might have expected from the partisanship of their districts. At least for Republicans in the Assembly class of 1986, it appears that new members before term limits were noticeably more extremist than veterans.

This pattern is not apparent for the Assembly class of 1996 (Figure 4.6). The parties are again highly polarized, although there are three Assemblymembers with centrist voting records in 1997.[10] New Democratic members are quite likely to have 100 percent AFL-CIO scores, just like the veterans of their caucus. The Democrats who did not always side with labor are from the more competitive districts, and in most cases, they are more moderate than veterans who represent similar seats. If there is any difference between new and experienced Republicans, it is that the first-term members are more centrist on labor issues than the partisanship of their district would predict.

Finally, the Senate records show that the class of 1996 did not differ much from longtime Senators (Figure 4.7). Although the new Senate Democrats in that year had strongly pro-labor voting records, the overall lesson is that most members of the class of 1996 voted just as one might

[10]The three Assemblymembers with centrist AFL-CIO scores in 1997 are Republicans from Democrat-leaning districts: Peter Frusetta (58%), Jim Morrisey (52%), and Jim Cuneen (39%).

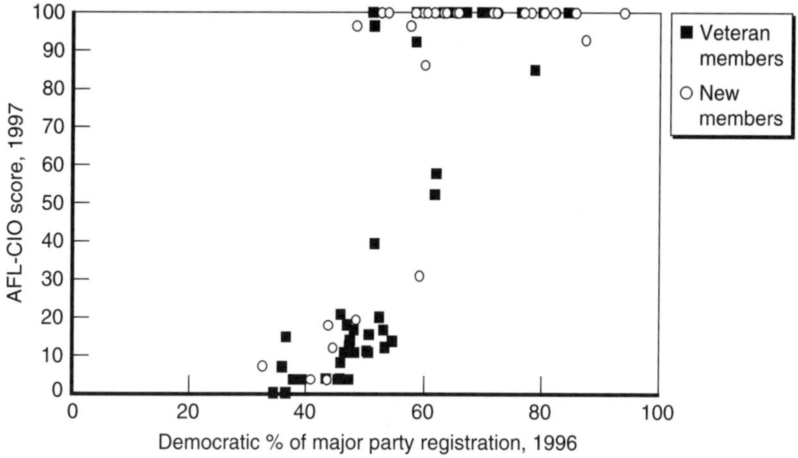

Data collected from the AFL-CIO's legislative reports, the California Secretary of State's Office, and Masket (2002) by Matt Tokeshi.

Figure 4.6—Ideological Extremism in the Assembly Class of 1996

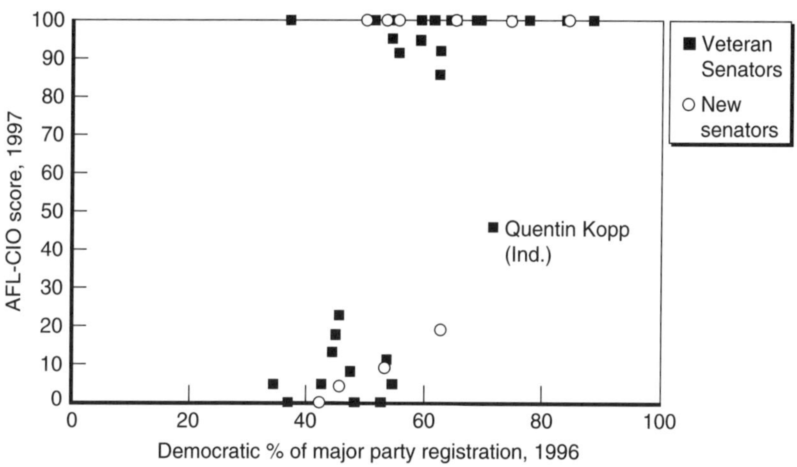

Data collected from the AFL-CIO's legislative reports and the California Secretary of State's Office, by Joseph Kim and Matt Tokeshi.

Figure 4.7—Ideological Extremism in the Senate Class of 1996

have predicted, given the composition of their districts. The relationship between party registration and AFL-CIO scores is roughly the same for new and old members, in both the Assembly and the Senate. These data provide no support for the assertion that term limits have led to the election of ideological extremists.

If there is a relationship between term limits and partisan polarization, then it must be found in the shifts in voting behavior of legislators over their careers. We have rejected one prediction that came from our first explanation—that new members are extremists—but perhaps the explanation is still correct that legislators drift toward the center as their time in Sacramento grows. Term limits may be cutting short a learning process that would otherwise make the Legislature as a whole more moderate. We test for the presence of this process by tracking the ideological trajectory of each class. Recording each member's voting record from each year that he or she served, we calculate a simple measure of extremity that is the absolute value of 50 percent minus a legislator's AFL-CIO score.[11] A middle-of-the-road member would have an ideological extremity score of 0, whereas a perfect partisan on either side of the aisle would receive a score of 50. This measure, proposed by research assistant Dan Enemark, allows us to combine data from members of both parties in both houses into a single line showing the extremity of the median member from each class in a given year.

The voting patterns of new members bounce up and down from year to year (Figure 4.8). This is almost certainly an election-year effect. The even years in this chart represent years in which all Assemblymembers and half the Senators face reelection, except for the class of 1996 in its final term. Quite predictably, the median legislator from each class has a

---

[11]We are able to use this simple measure—rather than one that considers the party registration in a district—because we are comparing each member's behavior from session to session rather than comparing different members in the same session. This comparison effectively holds a legislator's district constant. The only exception is that when many legislators drop out of our dataset in the later years, we are no longer comparing members from the same districts. We address this issue explicitly in our analysis.

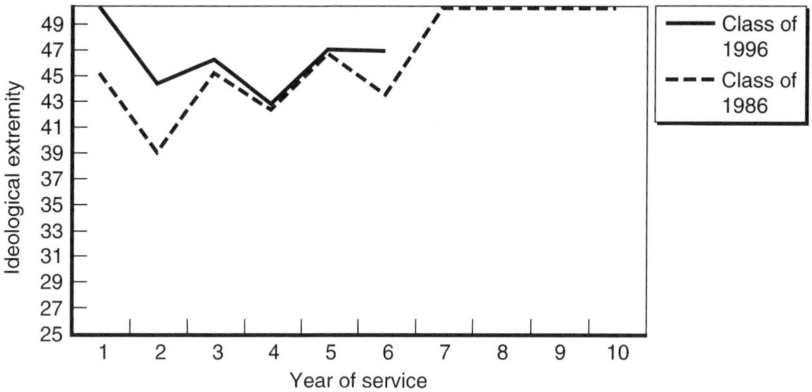

Data collected from the AFL–CIO's legislative reports and from Masket (2002) by Dan Enemark, Drew Cross, and Joseph Kim, and analyzed by Dan Enemark.

Figure 4.8—Ideological Trajectories Over the Careers of New Members

more moderate voting record during election years than in previous years. The only exceptions to this pattern are for the class of 1996 in its sixth year, when all Assemblymembers were termed out, and for the class of 1986 in years eight and ten. (All Assemblymembers remaining from this class were termed out in year ten.) Legislators appear to vote in a more centrist manner as elections near, except when term limits free them from immediate electoral pressures.

After sharp sophomore year corrections, legislators appear to grow more extreme in their voting behavior over time. Part of this pattern can be explained by the composition of our dataset. In years seven through ten, almost all the remaining members of the class of 1986 were staunch partisans from safe districts. The moderates from competitive seats were eliminated from the Legislature and thus from our analysis. This trend is also apparent in years three through six, however, when both classes were largely intact; approximately 75 percent of the class of 1986 and 68 percent of the class of 1996 stayed in their seats for at least six years. Just as they did before term limits, legislators in the post-Proposition 140 era drift *away from the center* through their careers. Rather than halting a centrist drift, term limits may in fact remove members before they become solid "yes" or "no" votes on such key issues as labor bills.

Why should legislators drift toward the extremes over their careers? One reviewer of this report suggested that veteran members become more closely associated with their party, seeking to enhance its reputation and to improve their own standing within it by voting the party line more frequently. Another pointed to the increased importance of doing well in party primaries as legislators seek to prolong their careers and move up to higher office. Whatever the reasons, California's legislators appear to drift toward the extremes over the years.

What is the overall effect of term limits on partisan polarization in California? We find no evidence that term limits have led to the election of ideological extremists. Comparing the voting records of new members in their first year to those of veterans, and controlling for the partisan makeup of districts, we see little change in the character of newly elected legislators. In fact, the 1986 Assembly class may have been slightly more polarized than the class of 1996. Further, term limits may make the Legislature as a whole more moderate by halting the extremist drift that most members appear to experience over their careers. The sole polarizing effect of Proposition 140 comes when members are termed out of a house; in their final session, they are freed from the electoral pressures that would otherwise push them toward the center. Our examination of individual voting records shows that the California Legislature has indeed become more polarized since the initiative was adopted but that term limits are not to blame.

5. Oversight of the Executive Branch

A major goal of the Legislature's 30-year effort to improve its level of professionalism—initiated by the Jesse Unruh-backed Proposition 1A that led to longer sessions, higher salaries, and a larger staff—was to make itself a co-equal branch of government (Bell and Price 1980, pp. 187–192). Governors have long had the opportunity to dominate state politics. More popular and visible than legislators, able to speak with a single voice, allowed to veto legislation and to "line item" spending proposals, and in control of the vast machinery of state government, the head of the executive branch possesses distinct institutional advantages (Rosenthal, 1990). California's governors have the first opportunity to propose a spending plan, and this advantage can be vital if legislators do not invest significant time in rewriting the state budget. A great deal of investigative effort is required of the Legislature to determine whether the bureaucracy is implementing state laws with appropriate vigor. If there is malfeasance within the executive branch, it will be revealed only if the Legislature is sufficiently energetic in its oversight.

Have term limits compromised the Legislature's ability to employ its informal tools to counter the governor's formal powers? Many scholars and political insiders fear that they have. "Oversight has suffered greatly since term limits," admits one Assembly chair. "The impact is due to the culture in the Legislature—it's a bill factory where members are looking to make a mark or leave a legacy or get district benefits. . . . There isn't enough time for the individual member to ride herd on the bureaucracy to implement bills."[1] A Senate chair points out a different dynamic that explains the same trend in the upper house. "The bureaucracies know

[1]Telephone interview by Bruce Cain and Thad Kousser, June 20, 2003, recorded by Ann Bordetsky.

that they can wait us out," she observes. "They stall or don't implement what we tell them to do because they know we won't be around."[2]

Term limits can erase the institutional memory necessary to scrutinize bureaucratic actions effectively. It takes time for new members to decide which executive policies they would like to change and which processes can best be used to change them. This loss of memory is not yet complete; many longtime members termed out of the Assembly in 1996 were elected to the Senate and will remain there until November 2004. The full effect of term limits on institutional memory will not be felt until such members as John Burton, Jim Brulte, John Vasconcellos, and Ross Johnson leave the Legislature. But by shortening the time horizons of all members, term limits reduce incentives to devote energy to oversight. If legislators do not foresee a lengthy career in state government, they may choose not to spend precious hours uncovering and fixing its problems. Similarly, they may not wish to sacrifice time and energy to defend the prerogatives of the legislative branch. Finally, the reduction in the size and expertise of legislative staff brought by Proposition 140 has denied the Legislature a critical resource in its struggle to become a co-equal branch.

This chapter examines the effects of term limits in three critical areas of the relationship between the legislative and executive branches of California state government. First and most important is the process of negotiation over the state budget. Looking closely at line items from four budgets written during comparable sessions, we find that the Legislature has made roughly 50 percent fewer amendments to the governor's budget since the implementation of term limits. Second, this pattern holds when we measure the Legislature's everyday oversight efforts through such activities as mandating audits and requesting budget information. Finally, a case study of the Legislature's investigation of Insurance Commissioner Charles Quackenbush identifies an instance of successful post-term limits oversight but shows that the reasons for success were quite particular to this case. Taken together, these findings suggest that term limits may usher in a new era of executive dominance in California politics.

---

[2]Interview by Karl Kurtz, Sacramento, California, February 26, 2002.

Budget Negotiations

> The governor will usually be an experienced politician and have more media exposure. Willie Brown could hold his own with [Governor George] Deukmejian and [Governor Pete] Wilson, but because leadership will turn over every few years, they are at a disadvantage. This adds to the power of a governor who already has constitutional powers.
>
> — Legislative staff member who formerly worked in the executive branch.[3]

> On the budget, members will be much more interested in their pork after term limits, because they don't have time there to do something tangible on the bigger scale. They are much more susceptible to getting picked off with pork.
>
> — Legislative staff member.[4]

The most powerful weapon that the California Legislature possesses in its frequent battles with governors is its ability to tighten—or to loosen—the state's purse strings. The budget process gives it an annual opportunity to exercise this power. Negotiations over how much to spend on thousands of budget items are regularly scheduled, well-documented contests between the executive branch and the Legislature. Budget battles therefore provide political scientists with ideal opportunities to study relations between the two branches. Our investigation of oversight begins by recording how active the Legislature has been in rewriting governors' budget proposals, and we find that term limits have sharply curtailed the Legislature's ability to have an independent voice in the budget process.

We considered a number of ways to measure the Legislature's power over the budget. One option was to compare how a governor divided up the budgetary "pie" among nine or ten major program areas to the final division that the Legislature and governor agreed to that year. This can be done fairly quickly over a number of years to give a comprehensive

[3]Telephone interview by Thad Kousser, August 2001.

[4]Telephone interview by Thad Kousser, August 2001.

view of budget bargaining in the pre- and post-term limits eras.[5] By ignoring the devilish details of budgets, however, this approach misses much of the real action. Members of budget committees have hundreds or even thousands of opportunities to alter the way that money is spent in large program areas, and this is where the Legislature can exercise real power.

Because legislators can make many consequential changes to a governor's program proposals without significantly changing total spending in those areas, we elected to look at budgets at the finest level of detail preserved in official documents: "program requirement items." An ideal research strategy would record every item in a governor's budget and compare it with the amount that the Legislature finally passed for that item. Unfortunately, the data-gathering requirements make this approach infeasible for a study of multiple budget negotiations. To compare the outcomes of legislative and executive conflicts before and after term limits, we identified three key program areas to track over four budget cycles.

We selected health care, higher education, and business services.[6] In each area, state officials exercise considerable discretion over spending levels, and they are not driven entirely by caseload shifts or governed by initiatives that tie the hands of policymakers.[7] Both governors and the

---

[5]In a pilot study conducted for this project, Kang (2001) compiled program-area budget figures over 20 years. She found no clear effect brought by term limits in the changes made by the Legislature to the aggregate funding levels proposed by the executive branch.

[6]We define higher education programs as the University of California, Hastings College of Law, the California State University, the California Maritime Academy, California Community Colleges, and the Student Aid Commission. Health care funding in California, under our definition, went toward the Emergency Medical Services Authority, the Office of Statewide Health Planning and Development, and the many programs of the Department of Health Services. Business services covers the Department of Alcoholic Beverage Control, the Department of Corporations, and the Department of Economic and Business Development (which later became the Department of Commerce and then the Trade and Commerce Agency).

[7]Prison spending and welfare (before 1997) are examples of areas where spending is tied to caseloads. Primary education is an example of an area governed by initiative: Proposition 98 mandated that a minimum percentage of new revenue sources in California be devoted to K–12 education. The initiative also applies to community college spending in California, which we include in higher education. Yet state

Legislature have the ability to set expenditures at levels that match their preferences. These areas reflect some of the breadth of a state government's responsibilities and are supported by different constituencies and parties. Excluding other areas of the budget from our analysis may obscure how negotiators make tradeoffs across issues, but it is unlikely to bias our findings about the effects of term limits.[8]

This analysis looks at four budgets written in the four sessions we introduced in Chapter 3. Matching the 1980–1981 fiscal year budget with the 2000–2001 spending plan allows us to observe legislative oversight during eras of unified government. Democratic-majority Legislatures negotiated with Democrat Jerry Brown over the second budget of his second term in 1980 and with Democrat Gray Davis over the second budget of his first term in 2000. Both budgets were written during years of significant fiscal expansion. General Fund spending in 1980–1981 was 13.3 percent higher than in the previous fiscal year, whereas expenditures grew by 17.4 percent between the 1999–2000 and the 2000–2001 budgets.[9] Democrats also controlled both houses of the Legislature when budgets for the 1987–1988 and 1997–1998 fiscal years were written. California government was divided, however, in each of these sessions. Republican Governor George Deukmejian was beginning his second term in 1987 and Republican Pete Wilson was nearing the

---

policymakers retain considerable control over the level of community college expenditures because they can trade them off against K–12 spending and still remain above the floor for educational spending required by the initiative. In health care, the state exercises significant discretion over MediCal and Healthy Families eligibility, which services will be provided, and how much doctors will receive for those services.

[8]For our findings on term limits to be biased, the following would have to occur: In both budgets that we look at in the pre-term limits era, governors would have to give the Legislature a relatively free hand to alter their proposals in health care, higher education, and business services in exchange for promising not to change many of the executive's spending plans in other areas. In both of the post-term limits budgets, exactly the opposite would have to occur. These occurrences are highly improbable.

[9]Expenditure data are drawn from the Department of Finance's "Historical Data: General Fund Budget Summary" chart from the www.dof.ca.gov website. Although spending growth was strong in 1980–1981, the state was establishing a new fiscal relationship with local governments to counteract the revenue losses from Proposition 13. Tighter finances during this pre-term limits budget should result in the Legislature making fewer changes in 1980–1981 than during the flush year of 2000–2001. This development biases our results against the finding that term limits have led to less legislative oversight of the budget.

end of his second term in 1997. Spending growth was relatively sluggish in both periods, with state spending rising by 4.8 percent in the first of these budgets and by 7.7 percent in the second. We have also verified that the magnitude of the May Revision of budget figures did not change in a way that called our results into question.[10] These four cases give us two pairs of pre- and post-term limits budgets constructed under roughly similar political and fiscal circumstances.

Focusing on our three selected portions of the budget, we began by recording how much a governor proposed spending on a given budget item in January and then noted how much the final appropriation deviated from this figure. Looking through appropriate editions of the Governor's Budget for each cycle, we recorded General Fund spending levels from many "program requirements" tables. For instance, Governor Jerry Brown recommended spending about $1.78 million in General Fund money on the Hastings College of Law's "Instruction Program" during the 1980–1981 fiscal year.[11] By examining the funding history for this item in the next fiscal year's budget, we see that the final deal between the executive and legislative branches set spending on this item at about $1.98 million. This change altered the executive proposal by 10.8 percent of its final value. It was added to all of the other changes

[10]Each year, the governor presents a May Revision to his proposed budget, which depends on the actual tax revenues that flow to Sacramento by April 15. If the May Revisions were particularly large in our pre-term limits cases, this could provide an alternative explanation for the effect that we observe: The Legislature may have altered the governor's January proposals more in the pre-term limits era not because it was more activist but because it was responding to a larger May Revision. Fortunately, this is not the case. The change in total proposed General Fund spending after the May Revision was 2.6 percent in 1987–1988 and 2.8 percent in 1997–1998, remaining about constant. It was 0.2 percent in 1980–1981 but 13.7 percent in 2000–2001, a shift that suggests that we have in fact understated the effect of term limits on the Legislature's level of budget scrutiny.

[11]General Fund refers to the portion of money in a state's coffers that does not come from federal grants or from specialized state funds that are often dedicated to specific purposes. Because it is the source of funding over which California officials exercise unfettered control, we generally analyze General Fund spending exclusively in this analysis. To study some policy areas over time, however, we did not differentiate when General Funds were replaced by discretionary sources such as university general purpose funds, the Alcohol Beverage Control Fund, or the State Corporations Fund.

made to the governor's higher education, health care, and business services budgets in order to compute the totals reported in Figure 5.1.

In both pairs of comparable cases, the Legislature changed half as much of the governor's budget after term limits as it did before, and the legislative branch has become the least independent in health care (Table 5.1). The magnitude of this trend is the same under divided and unified government and represents billions of dollars in legislative discretion that is no longer exercised.[12] Kousser (2002c) finds that term limits have had the same effect on legislative amendments to executive budget proposals in Colorado, Maine, and Oregon, but that legislative power has increased in the non-term limits states of Illinois and New Mexico. In California as in other states, limiting the terms of legislators has limited their power in the budget-writing process.

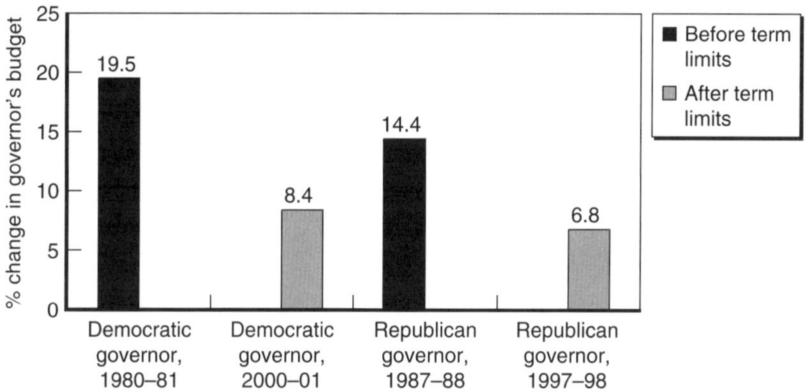

% change represents the ratio of the total line-by-line changes made by the Legislature to the total final appropriation levels in health care, higher education, and business services.

Figure 5.1—Changes Made to the Governor's Budget

---

[12]Counter to our intuition, changes made to the executive proposals were greater in eras of unified rather than divided government. This may be because these were also years of greater fiscal growth, giving the Legislature a larger surplus to play with. It also may be further evidence that the constitutional provision requiring a two-thirds vote in each house to pass a budget gives the legislative minority a remarkably powerful voice.

Table 5.1

Changes Made to Governor's Budget Proposal, by Year and Budget Area

Session	Budget Area	Total Final Spending in Budget Area	Total Changes Made to Governor's Request ($)	% Change
		Before Term Limits		
1980–1981	Higher education	3,113,849,522	240,669,631	7.7
	Health care	2,999,099,080	952,457,591	31.8
	Business services	31,451,288	2,318,911	7.4
1987–1988	Higher education	5,229,475,000	480,603,000	9.2
	Health care	4,081,365,000	866,905,000	21.2
	Business services	45,273,000	3,377,000	7.5
		After Term Limits		
1997–1998	Higher education	6,987,727,000	694,003,000	9.9
	Health care	7,275,325,000	271,075,000	3.7
	Business services	120,729,000	16,458,000	13.6
2000–2001	Higher education	9,965,866,000	799,725,000	8.0
	Health care	10,216,603,000	886,751,000	8.7
	Business services	164,759,000	29,460,000	17.9

Table entries represent the sum of changes made to many budget lines in each area.

Ongoing Oversight Activities

> In many ways, oversight is more significant than passing laws. . . . The passing of the law is an important event, but the implementation is vastly more important. Politicians don't get credit for oversight. It's the harder and less rewarding aspect of the work but it is a much more important function in terms of changing the world out there.
>
> — Veteran Senate committee consultant.[13]

> I think one of the things you're losing with a term-limited legislature is that the institutional role and knowledge of program are being lost and will not be gained in the Assembly.
>
> — Former Senate budget advisor Fred Silva (2001).

> The Assembly is now talking about revamping the oversight process, but members don't know the existing process. They don't know the difference

[13]Interview by Ann Bordetsky and Lori Kim, Sacramento, California, Spring 2002.

> between the Legislative Analyst's Office, the California Research Bureau, the Department of Finance, and so on. They don't know when it is appropriate to ask a department, a public stakeholder, or the LAO to testify. They grill the wrong people for the wrong information during hearings. . . . The Legislature is like the Board of Directors for a company that doesn't know anything about the company.
>
> — Former Assembly staff member who later worked in the executive branch.[14]

Although each summer's budget negotiations provide high-profile conflicts between the legislative and executive branches of government, insiders point to the mundane tasks of everyday oversight as an equally important part of the Legislature's prerogatives. These oversight duties can take many forms. Legislators can request that professional staff organizations, such as the Bureau of State Audits, produce reports on the activities of the executive branch. Committee chairs can hold hearings, often during the interim between active sessions, to investigate an issue or call agency representatives for questioning. During any type of hearing, committee members may question executive liaisons about the implementation of bills or budget items. Legislative staff—most often committee consultants—may communicate with their contacts within a state bureaucracy to check on its performance. Whistle-blowers in an agency may decide on their own to contact legislators or staff. Quite often, interest groups will educate the Legislature about the actual practices of state agencies.

We would like to measure the frequency of all of these activities before and after term limits. However, because of the sometimes secretive nature of oversight, only the formal oversight activities leave an available paper trail. This section presents quantitative records of two ways in which the Legislature can keep tabs on the executive branch: by inserting requests into the Legislative Analyst Office's "Supplemental Report to the Budget Bill" and by asking for Bureau of State Audit reports (Bordetsky and Kim, 2002). The frequency of both of these actions can be recorded, and we present a time series for each that spans

[14]Interview by Ann Bordetsky, Sacramento, California, May 2, 2003.

the passage of Proposition 140 and the implementation of term limits. We find quantitative evidence that the Legislature has become less active in its ongoing oversight of the executive branch since the advent of term limits.

Our first measure of oversight takes as its source the "Supplemental Report to the Budget Bill," an annual document published by the LAO. This report compiles requests by the Legislature to have executive agencies provide them with information along with statements that reiterate the statutory or budgetary mandates given to certain departments. It is the written record of the Legislature's intent on oversight matters. Although the requests are not binding, they represent an important, quantifiable record of the body's annual attempts at oversight.

Adding up the number of requests in 17 budget cycles, beginning with the LAO's supplement for the 1985–1986 fiscal year, Figure 5.2 traces budget oversight in recent times. It suggests that term limits brought a steep decline in the number of requests for agency information. Their annual frequency dropped from a mean of 199.2 in 1985–1990 to 118.8 in the first six supplement reports issued after passage of the term limits initiative. Over this period, veteran legislators

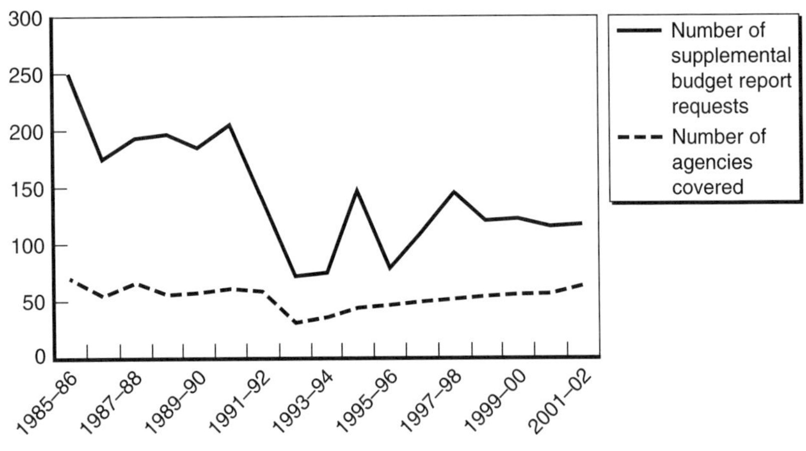

Figure 5.2—Frequency and Scope of Supplemental Budget Requests

remained in Sacramento but expected their careers to end soon, with the first large group of casualties coming in 1996. It is likely that with their time horizons shortened, these veterans paid less attention to the unglamorous tasks of oversight. When long-time legislators began to be replaced by new members—energetic but unfamiliar with traditional modes of oversight—between 1996 and 2002, the Legislature made an average of 120.7 requests per year. The difference between the average number of reports before Proposition 140's passage and its mean after passage is significant at the 95 percent confidence level.

The number of agencies covered by these requests took a slight dip at the same time that the number of requests fell. The average number of agencies covered declined from 60.6 agencies until 1990 to 50.7 after the passage of Proposition 140, a difference that is again significant at the 95 percent confidence level. Although there has been little change in its scope, the frequency of legislative oversight through the LAO's "Supplemental Report to the Budget Bill" has decreased dramatically.

Next, we look at the Bureau of State Audits (BSA) reports requested by the Legislature that evaluate the use of state funds by executive branch departments. Individual legislators can ask for audits, but the Joint Legislative Audit Committee must clear their requests. Because completed reports become part of the public record, we can count the reports completed each year and measure their scope. Responsibility for this type of audit was transferred from the Auditor General's Office to the Bureau of State Audits in 1993. Because of this, the number of audits completed in that year was atypically low, and we exclude 1993 data from our analysis. Because the nature of the audits did not change during this transfer, however, we believe that our comparisons of the pre- and post-term limits eras are valid.

The number of BSA reports requested by the Legislature declined sharply just after Proposition 140 passed, stayed low when veteran members remained in Sacramento but abandoned their plans for a long career of state service, and increased between 1997 and 2001 (Figure 5.3). It seems that the new generation of legislators brought by term limits has learned how to use the BSA to conduct oversight and has found this investment worthwhile.

Along with this comforting evidence that legislative oversight has rebounded, however, come signals that BSA reports may not be as powerful a tool as they were before term limits. The number of audits completed before the start of the next fiscal year, and thus especially useful for budget oversight, declined in the early 1990s and has yet to rebound. Before the passage of Proposition 140, 58.8 percent of reports were completed before July, but an average of only 44.5 percent of them have been finished by this month in each year since 1996. Because this difference is not significant at the 95 percent confidence level, firm conclusions cannot yet be drawn from the apparent trend.

The scope of BSA audits has also narrowed (Figure 5.4). The number of departments audited by each year's set of reports and the number of statewide issues that they address (rather than questions concerning agency activities in a single county) fell in the early 1990s and has not yet returned to pre-term limits levels.

Data collected from Bureau of State Audits records by Ann Bordetsky.

Figure 5.3—Frequency and Timing of BSA Reports

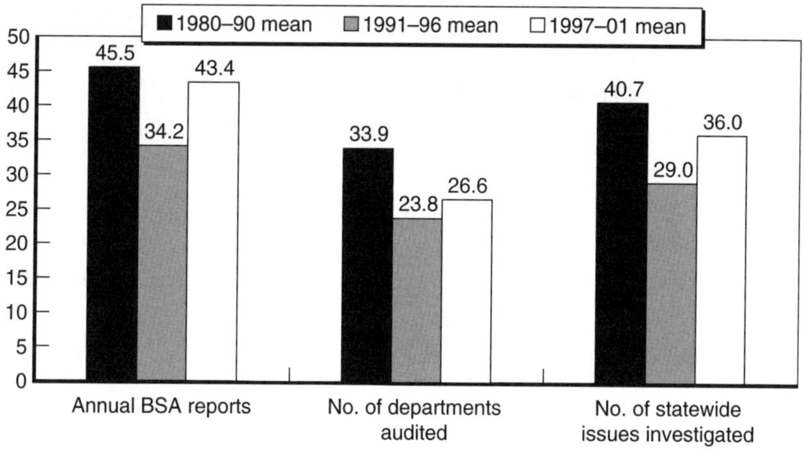

Data collected from Bureau of State Audits records by Ann Bordetsky.

Figure 5.4—Number and Scope of BSA Reports

Case Study of the Quackenbush Investigation

To complement our quantitative measures of the Legislature's ability to monitor and influence the executive branch, we present a brief qualitative account of the effects of term limits on oversight. Oversight is a difficult subject to analyze using the case study approach. Picking one high-profile case of successful oversight can present a misleading picture, highlighting an atypical triumph and thus overstating the Legislature's ability to identify and end bureaucratic misbehavior. Likewise, agencies may have thwarted the Legislature's will repeatedly, but if members did not notice these activities, none of them could become a case study of oversight failure. Instead of arguing that a case study can illuminate changes in the overall pattern of oversight brought by term limits, we use this section to look closely at the nature of oversight after Proposition 140. We attempt to identify the strengths that the Legislature used to compensate for its lack of experience and altered incentives. We also judge whether a case of effective oversight today is likely to be repeated, or whether it may be a singular event.

Our case is often identified as the crowning achievement of post-term limits oversight: the Legislature's investigation of Insurance Commissioner Charles Quackenbush.[15] After recounting the events that led to Quackenbush's resignation, we consider why the Legislature could delve so successfully into secretive executive branch behavior in this case. We find that its success was highly dependent on specific conditions and legislators. Many of these legislators are now gone and not likely to be replaced by members with similar strengths and interests. Although it is difficult to draw firm conclusions from a single case study, the Quackenbush investigation suggests that the Legislature can perform good oversight after term limits but only when the conditions are ripe.

On November 4, 1999, a concerned Woodland Hills resident called the staff of the Senate Insurance Committee to ask how Insurance Commissioner Chuck Quackenbush was paying for public service announcements in which he was featured prominently. Since the 1994 Northridge earthquake, homeowners in the San Fernando Valley had been asking state regulators for help with what they considered to be mishandled insurance claims. Now Quackenbush, who had not taken a particularly hard line against the insurers for their post-quake payouts, was appearing on their television sets. Committee staff began to investigate the nonprofit foundation that funded the ads, the "California Research and Assistance Fund (CRAF)." Unable to examine the documents that detailed Department of Insurance expenditures on CRAF, Senate Insurance Chair Jackie Speier asked Attorney General Bill Lockyer to audit the foundation on January 27, 2000. The Assembly Insurance Committee began an investigation of its own, notifying the Department of Insurance on March 24 that it would conduct oversight hearings on the matter.[16]

---

[15]Although this investigation has been widely hailed as a success, it is not the only example of post-term limits oversight. The Legislature's investigations of Oracle contributions to Governor Gray Davis and of pricing practices in the electricity and natural gas markets have also garnered praise.

[16]Information in this paragraph and the following one comes from interviews with Senate and Assembly Insurance Committee staff conducted by Ann Bordetsky by telephone and in Sacramento, California, in the summer of 2003.

The story went public two days later when the *Los Angeles Times* published the first in a series of investigative pieces written by veteran Sacramento journalist Virginia Ellis. Ellis's story detailed $245,000 in political contributions that insurance companies made to Quackenbush's campaign fund shortly after the department decided not to fine the companies for unfair claim practices in the wake of the 1994 quake (Ellis, 2000a). Some of these funds were then transferred into the campaign account of Kris Quackenbush, the insurance commissioner's wife, to repay a personal loan that she made to her failed 1998 State Senate candidacy (Lucas, 2000). Ellis published a report a week later showing that the companies had also funded the CRAF (Ellis, 2000b). The Insurance Committees in both houses began to hold hearings, with the Assembly meeting on April 27 and the Senate insurance committee traveling to Granada Hills on May 10 to hear complaints from dissatisfied claimants.

Subpoenaed by the Senate committee, Chuck Quackenbush appeared before it on June 5, 2000, and many of his staff members testified before the Assembly Insurance Committee throughout that month. The investigation eventually showed that department staff had recommended levying more than $3 billion worth of fines against insurers and ordering them to pay $233 million to policyholders (Lucas, 2000). Yet only a single insurer, 20th Century, was fined, and only in the amount of $100,000. Along with State Farm and Allstate, 20th Century donated $11 million to the CRAF, $3 million of which was used to air public service announcements starring Quackenbush. These discoveries forced Deputy Insurance Commissioner George Grays, who managed the CRAF, to resign on April 14 (*Associated Press*, 2000; Squatrigilia, 2000). The June oversight hearings focused on Quackenbush's knowledge of the links between insurers and the CRAF, and he resigned on July 10, 2000.

How did the Legislature probe and conclude this episode of executive branch malfeasance? First, the investigation itself was a reaction to a constituent inquiry and subsequent media reports. Although donations to Quackenbush's campaign had been reported in 1999, it took an outside inquiry to point committee staff toward this scandal. This may indicate a pattern of post-term limits oversight investigations reacting to outside discoveries rather than stemming from proactive policing of the bureaucracy.

Second, many observers credit the exemplary leadership shown by individual legislators with the success of the investigation. The Assembly oversight hearings worked, said one staffer involved, "because of a fortuitous coming together of talented people. . . . Fred Keeley was perfect for the Quackenbush era."[17] A Democratic member of the Assembly Insurance Committee and close ally of Speaker Robert Hertzberg, Keeley was one of the investigation's informal leaders. Assembly and Senate Insurance Chairs Scott and Speier drew praise for convening thorough, evenhanded hearings. Democrat Darrell Steinberg, Assembly Insurance Vice-Chair Ken Maddox, and Republican Tom McClintock distinguished themselves as well.

Many of these members were Sacramento veterans of the type that will be eliminated soon by term limits. Speier served in the Assembly from 1986–1996 and was first elected to the Senate in 1998. Although Keeley did not become an Assemblyman until 1996, he was a longtime Sacramento staffer who used his knowledge of state government and the legislative process to great acclaim in the Quackenbush affair. First elected to the Assembly in 1982 at age 26, Tom McClintock had served for five years in the Republican leadership and had already made one run for statewide office. Although Scott, Maddox, and Steinberg are all examples of fresh, bright members who came to Sacramento after the implementation of Proposition 140, many major figures of the Quackenbush inquiry were holdovers from the pre-term limits era.

Many interviewees pointed out a third secret of the investigation's success: the Assembly leadership's interest in oversight and willingness to devote resources to the cause. "Top-down influence accounts for the Quackenbush investigation's success," concluded a member of the Assembly Insurance Committee. "The Speaker made oversight a priority and invested the resources in order to professionalize it. He hired outside counsel, outside investigators to look into every aspect."[18] The

---

[17]Interview by Ann Bordetsky, Sacramento, California, June 23, 2003.

[18]Telephone interview by Bruce Cain and Thad Kousser, June 20, 2003, recorded by Ann Bordetsky.

Assembly Insurance Committee hired Matthew Jacobs, who had conducted white-collar crime investigations at the U.S. Attorney's Office, to provide legal advice and guide the interviews of Department of Insurance staff.[19] "Matt Jacobs gave the Assembly credibility and clout that wouldn't have come without legal counsel. . . . None of the members had been through anything like that," recounted another staff member.[20] Although the division of resources was not absolutely even, the Assembly leadership provided Republicans funds for staff that a Republican member of the Assembly Insurance Committee described as "helpful in promoting bipartisanship."[21]

The temporary infusion of resources after a politically helpful story had already broken does not guarantee that this sort of support for oversight will continue. When Speaker Hertzberg was termed out in November 2002, the Office of Oversight that he had created "got lost in the shuffle of new Speakers."[22] When asked whether Hertzberg's legacy of commitment to oversight persists, one member involved in the investigation replied, "The training institute and investigation leave a legacy, but they have not resulted in an institutionalized process yet."

Conclusion

New legislators face significant obstacles in their efforts to oversee the executive branch. Lacking their predecessors' experience in Sacramento, they do not have the tools to easily discover and attack bureaucratic wrongdoing. Their incentives to pass legislation quickly may outweigh their incentives to see that these bills are implemented in the ways that they intend. Because they do not anticipate a long future in the legislative branch, they have little reason to defend its independence from the executive branch. And because many members reach positions of real power for only a budget cycle or two, agency officials can sometimes wait them out.

---

[19]Telephone interview by Bruce Cain, July 14, 2003, recorded by Ann Bordetsky.

[20]Interview by Ann Bordetsky, Sacramento, California, June 23, 2003.

[21]Telephone interview by Bruce Cain and Ann Bordetsky, June 20, 2003, recorded by Ann Bordetsky.

[22]Telephone interview by Bruce Cain, July 14, 2003, recorded by Ann Bordetsky.

The effects of these obstacles on legislative oversight are borne out in our quantitative investigations of oversight activity. Comparing two budgets written before 1990 with two spending plans written in similar sessions after Proposition 140 suggests a dramatic decline in the Legislature's budgeting power. Legislators today alter about half as much of the governor's proposed expenditures as their counterparts did before term limits. The Legislature's ongoing oversight activities, as measured by the frequency of supplemental budget requests and by the number and scope of audits ordered by members, have also declined. Looking closely at one case of successful oversight after term limits, the Quackenbush investigation, we find some encouraging signs that executive wrongdoing can still be discovered. Yet the major reasons for the success of this inquiry are highly dependent upon the particular personalities of those involved—many of whom are now termed out. Overall, Proposition 140 has weakened the Legislature's ability to bargain with and oversee the executive branch, which is perhaps the initiative's most troubling effect.

6. Adapting to Term Limits

Very few state legislators and staff, including those who succeeded termed-out incumbents, believe that term limits have improved the Legislature. Even so, there is little likelihood that California voters will eliminate them in the near future. Unless public opinion on this issue changes, a more constructive alternative to the ongoing debate about the wisdom of term limits is to ask how the Legislature can best function under their constraints. Our assumption throughout this discussion is that voters did not seek to destroy legislative capacity when they approved Proposition 140. Rather, we assume that they hoped for more turnover and legislative competence at the same time.

Our study has revealed several ways that the Legislature has adapted to term limits. Consider, for instance, the role of a two-chambered Legislature in the post-term limits era. During the constitutional revision deliberations of the mid-1990s, there was serious discussion of reducing the Legislature to one house. Bicameralism made sense, some argued, before the "one person, one vote" decisions in the 1960s, largely because one house was based on population and the other on geographical units (e.g., counties) in the so-called "federal model." When the State Senate seats were changed to the same equal population standard used for Assembly districts, however, and especially when two Assembly seats were "nested" into one Senate seat under the two Court Masters' plans, there was little difference in the interests represented by the two houses. Indeed, Brady and Gaines (1995) found little difference in the voting patterns in the two houses after the reapportionment revolution. At the same time, conference committees reconciling bills passed in the two houses often became arenas for last-minute skullduggery. This outcome led experienced legislators such as Lucy Killea and Barry Keene to conclude that either a unicameral legislature (on the model of Nebraska) or a parliamentary system (such as in Britain) would be preferable to the current arrangement.

Term limits, however, have given bicameralism a new reason for existence. The lower house is the entry point and the training ground for most new legislators, whereas the upper house serves as the more experienced counterbalance. Evidence for this can be found in the comparative experience levels of committee chairs and senior staff as well as in amendment activities in the two houses. This sort of compensation—that is, Senate experience offsetting Assembly turnover—was not planned or mandated by Proposition 140. It happened naturally as legislators pursued a logical career path from the Assembly to the Senate. When the last of pre-1990 members leave the Senate in 2004, the experience gap between the two houses should diminish somewhat and possibly decrease differences between the Senate and Assembly in the future.

Legislators have also learned that they need to mix experienced staff with campaign loyalists. Representatives who filled their Sacramento offices with novices quickly found themselves at a disadvantage and relied heavily on lobbyists for expertise and guidance. But conventional wisdom soon corrected this flaw. Other adaptations occurred by accident. For instance, we found that inexperienced Senate committee chairs were often paired with more experienced committee staff. When we asked whether this sort of pairing was intentional, we discovered that it was instead the artifact of less prestigious committees often having more stable staff (i.e., because there was less competition for these positions). As a result, new Senators on less prestigious committees inherited more experienced staff.

Aside from these natural adaptations, what more can the Legislature do to increase its effectiveness under term limits? We explore three areas: staff and member training, budget activity, and alterations to California's term limit law.

Staff and Member Training

Member turnover has led to greater staff turnover. As new members replace termed-out incumbents, they bring new staff into the process. As they move from the Assembly to the Senate, legislators take their experienced staff with them, perpetuating the imbalance in experience between the two houses. The Senate then tends to override the

Assembly on legislative matters, causing unnecessary tension between the two houses. One solution is to mix more experienced staff with new staff. The Assembly might accomplish this through changes in personnel policies or salary levels. In recent years, this has also meant retaining a stable of experienced staff in the Assembly Speaker's Office or in the majority caucus offices. These experienced staff apparently shadow and monitor the less experienced committee and personal staffs.

The model of experienced staff advising less experienced legislators is familiar to legislators with experience in local government. The Unruh-era concept of a professionalized, nonpartisan policy staff is similar to the city manager model in local government. Since those days, legislative staffers have become more partisan, and the Legislature will likely continue to build its experienced staff corps within the party caucuses. Still, the need for neutral expertise is apparent. Almost everyone we interviewed noted that the bill drafters in the Legislative Counsel and the policy analysts in the Legislative Analyst's Office had important functions in the term limits era.

Even with a determined effort to keep experienced staff, however, staff turnover will persist, and the Legislature needs an effective way to train new staff. Under Speaker Robert Hertzberg, the Assembly took steps in this direction by establishing its C.A.P.I.T.O.L. Institute. Speaker Hertzberg also developed manuals and documents that would make a permanent record of received legislative wisdom and practices. Staff members and legislators we interviewed believed that this program was a welcome addition.

For the most part, legislators attended only the first C.A.P.I.T.O.L. sessions, in which they learned how to set up staff and deal with travel, facilities, and Assembly publications and resources. They received some process and ethics training and heard presentations about the committees. The sessions also allowed legislators to introduce themselves to one another. There were subsequent training sessions on bill writing and the budget, but most legislators preferred to learn about these aspects of their job more informally from peer mentors. One legislator told us that the really valuable information about legislative tactics and how to deal with other members came from conversations with more senior members. Another, a Republican, said that the institute did nothing to overcome the forces of partisanship because "partisanship results from the issues, not the presence or absence of personal bonds."

For staff, formal training is clearly very important and should be continued. Some of the current topics in the C.A.P.I.T.O.L. training include the budget process, how to staff legislation, training to be a Chief of Staff, practical management issues, scheduling tips, constituent casework, and techniques for field representatives. Legislative and budgetary training are critical on the Assembly side. The more training staff have on these matters, the less the legislator's office as a whole must depend on lobbyists and outsiders to provide expertise and knowledge.

This training may even be able to affect the content of the legislation coming out of the Assembly. Several State Senators and staff complained that Assembly bills often did not do what they were intended to do and therefore had to be amended constantly. We also found a decline in gatekeeping by the Assembly committees and that their bills are more subject to amendment and changes on the floor. This can lead to complex and messy legislation. Has the training helped in this regard?

To answer this question, we employed two measures developed in previous chapters. First, we compared the so-called legislative batting averages of the classes of 1996 (i.e., pre-C.A.P.I.T.O.L. Institute training) and 1998 (those who received the C.A.P.I.T.O.L. training), separating the scores of each party. The differences are very small (Figure 6.1). Democratic scores go up slightly and Republican scores go down, but not by appreciable amounts. On this measure, it is hard to see that an expanded training program has made any real difference. A look at enrolled bills (which would not be affected as much by the change in the governorship) shows no improvement in batting averages, either.

Another possibility is that the training affected the complexity of legislation. Using a sample of legislative histories of 136 bills over four legislative sessions, we computed the average number of lines, sections, and codes affected by the bills passed in two pre-term limits sessions (1979–1980 and 1987–1988), a pre-C.A.P.I.T.O.L. training/post-term limits session (1997–1998), and a post-C.A.P.I.T.O.L. training/post-term limits session (1999–2000). Unlike the figures in Chapter 3, Figure 6.2 reports the breadth and complexity of bills authored by first-

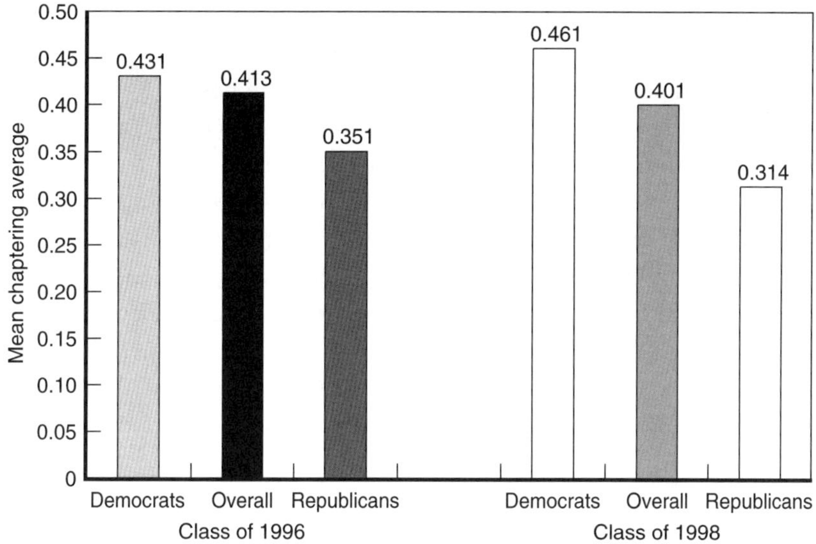

Data collected from bill histories by Matt Tokeshi, Cathy Ellis, and Tam Bui.

Figure 6.1—Batting Averages of the Classes of 1996 and 1998, Chaptered Bills

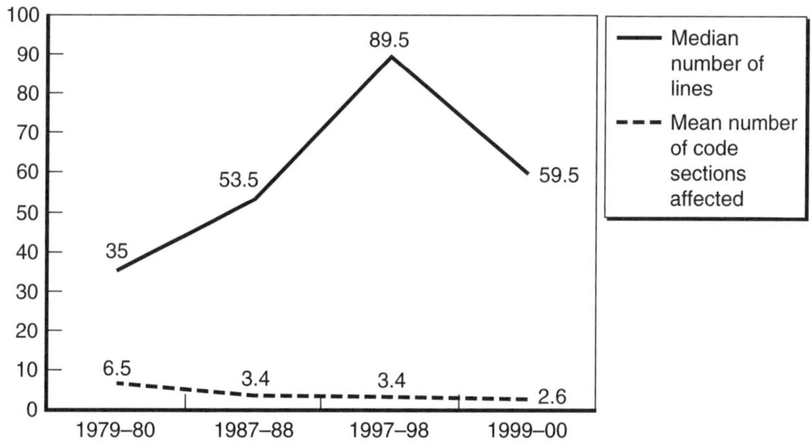

Data collected from the chaptered text of 136 bills by Natalie Freese.

Figure 6.2—Breadth and Complexity of Bills Passed by New Assemblymembers

term members only. The data indicate that freshman bills after term limits consumed more lines but affected fewer code sections. There is some reduction in complexity between the pre- and post-C.A.P.I.T.O.L. training periods. We cannot say for certain that the training helps explain this disparity, but that remains a possibility.

One clear weakness in the training is in the area of oversight. We have seen that term limits have reduced the amount of oversight activity as measured by the number of budgetary supplemental requests for information from state agencies and by requests for Bureau of State Audit reports. A failure to conduct effective oversight could result in more agency waste and less compliance. One way to improve the Legislature's oversight capacity would be to add more staff training in this area.

Budget Activity

Another area that needs improvement is the budget process. Lost in the discussion so far of how California found itself with a $38 billion deficit in 2003 is the breakdown of the budget process itself under term limits. We have seen that the Legislature's capacity to rewrite executive proposals has diminished sharply. In interviews with senior budget staff, we discovered that the budget process has broken down in other ways as well.

- Relatively little work is done now in budget subcommittees, which means that ideas are not tested until they reach conference committee. As a result, there is less transparency, less consensus to build on, more delays in the budget process, and more room for purely political deals.
- Subcommittees now rely less on the neutral expertise of the LAO. As one veteran budget staffer told us, "Now interest groups and lots of other folks can put things on the agenda. No one has done the research that needs to be done."
- Term-limited legislators tend to know less about the budget as a whole and care more about obtaining funds for specific projects and bills.

- Much of the subcommittee work must be based on preliminary numbers because actual tax revenues are not known until May. When revenue projections are particularly unstable, there is more pressure to do everything quickly at the end of the budget cycle.
- With the proliferations of trailer bills, many programs bypass the vetting of policy committees. As one staff person put it, "They get an up or down vote on the floor, but not much scrutiny . . . it is no longer acceptable to vote against another member's bill unless it's for a personal reason."
- Fiscal accountability depends on gatekeeping by budget committees that have overall spending and revenue targets in mind. This gatekeeping is missing in the current system.
- Members have voted for bills knowing that they would not be in the Legislature to deal with their negative consequences.

In short, there was reason to expect that a chaotic budget process—less transparent, lacking overall spending and revenue targets, and aimed at buying votes to pass a bill—would take longer to complete during tough times and would be fiscally irresponsible during good times.

The Legislature could take several measures to ensure more stability and responsibility in the budget process. First, the Legislature should consider holding more joint Senate-Assembly subcommittee hearings to work out agreements in specific funding areas. Second, these subcommittees should be given specific funding targets to work within to avoid a burgeoning, irresponsible budget. Third, proposals from each house's subcommittees should be reported under closed rules and not easily changed in the budget conference committee. This former practice of "locking" budget items on which both houses agreed should be reinstated to make subcommittee hearings more consequential. Fourth, the LAO should be strengthened, given a larger role, and staffed at previous levels. Fifth, chairs of the budget subcommittees should be members of the final budget conference committee to ensure that agreements made early on are adhered to more closely in the final stages.

These proposals may bring more consensus and fiscal accountability to the process. To be sure, the fiscal crisis in 2003 was primarily caused by the economic downturn, but spending soared during the prosperous years well beyond any prudent expectation of average revenue. The disjointed, opaque budget process and opportunistic mentality of term-limited legislators added significantly to the problem. Fixing the process could help prevent a repeat of the spending patterns of the late 1990s.

Modifying Term Limits

Our studies show that the committee system in the California Legislature is not working to develop the necessary expertise and institutional memory. Committee chairs and senior staff have significantly lower levels of experience and do not stay with committees for more than one term on average. This pattern has weakened gatekeeping, especially in the Assembly. Legislators have not taken their budget subcommittees seriously in recent years, and leaders, especially Assembly Speakers, have had little time to coordinate the agendas of diverse members or to build the institution as a whole before they are removed from their posts. All of these trends have weakened the Legislature as a branch of government, a decline that is especially apparent in budget negotiations with the governor.

It is hard to see how these problems can be corrected under the current system. The terms allowed under Proposition 140 are the shortest in the nation.[1] With a six-year limit in the Assembly and a need to make one's mark quickly, there is little incentive to stay with a policy area and master its details. There is even less incentive to do the routine work of oversight unless it can grab headlines, as the Quackenbush insurance scandal did.

There is little voter appetite for eliminating term limits, but it may be possible to modify the existing limits to provide for a total service limit rather than a specific one for each legislative house. Instead of

---

[1]Two other states—Arkansas and Michigan—share California's six-year term limit in their lower houses. Nine states have eight-year term limits in each house, and four states allow 12 years in each house. See the National Conference of State Legislatures (2004).

allowing legislators six years in the Assembly and eight in the Senate, a new provision could limit members to 14 years of total legislative service. Oklahoma's term-limit law has just such a "mix-and-match" provision. This alteration would do little to erode the gains brought by Proposition 140. The Legislature is already more diverse, and the oldest Senators have already been termed out. Because nearly every Senator today is a former Assemblymember, limiting total legislative service would not increase the average age or tenure in the Senate.

That change would be likely to increase Assembly tenures, however, and our findings suggest that this outcome may be beneficial. A mix-and-match provision would stem the flow from the Assembly into the Senate and allow legislators who stay in one house to learn more about particular policy areas and committees. Experience levels for Assembly chairs and consultants, which have dropped to very low levels, would rebound. Assembly committees could also perform their gatekeeping function more proficiently. Crucially, Assembly leaders and budget negotiators who chose not to run for the Senate would have more time to obtain expertise and lead their caucuses effectively. As a result, the Legislature as a whole could be strengthened in its budget negotiations and oversight action. This type of term-limit law would make the houses more equal in experience and the branches more equal in power even as it ensured the turnover required by Proposition 140.

Conclusion

Perhaps the best way to summarize our results is by comparing what we have found to the expectations of both the proponents and opponents of Proposition 140, as stated in their November 1990 ballot arguments. Many predictions centered on the effects of term limits on legislative careers and elections. Proponents claimed that Proposition 140 would "reform a political system that has created a legislature of career politicians." We find that term limits have altered the pattern of careerism rather than ending it. The typical career path now flows from the Assembly to the Senate and then to higher offices or to local government. A related claim was that term limits would "end the ingrown, political nature of both houses." We find that fewer former staffers have been elected, that more local government officials now run for the Assembly, and that the Senate consists predominantly of former Assemblymembers. The ballot argument in favor of Proposition 140 promised that it would "create more competitive elections" and claimed that "Incumbent legislators seldom lose . . . it is time to put an end to a system that makes incumbents a special class of citizens." Our review of the scholarly literature reveals that term limits have increased turnover but not competitiveness between parties. Even today, few incumbents lose until they are termed out, and their parties almost always retain their seats.

Proponents of Proposition 140 also wished to reform the internal operations of the Legislature. "By reducing the amount [that legislators] can spend on their personal office expenses," they claimed, "Proposition 140 will cut back on the 3,000 political staffers who serve the legislature." We show that legislators evaded the intent of this cut by eliminating positions for relatively expensive nonpartisan experts and keeping their political staffs. Another claim was that Proposition 140 would "remove the grip that special interests have over the legislature and remove the huge political slush funds at the disposal of Senate and Assembly leaders." Our analysis shows that patterns in fundraising from special interests have not changed since the initiative's passage, and those we interviewed told us that lobbyists still help many members draft and pass bills. One assertion of term limits backers has undeniably come true: "Proposition 140 will end the reign of the legislature's powerful officers—the Assembly Speaker (first elected a quarter of a century ago) and the Senate leader (now into his third decade as a legislator)." In fact, the initiative termed out these leaders and weakened legislative leadership more generally.

Opponents of Proposition 140 made their own predictions about the effects of term limits. "No matter how good a job someone does in office," they argued, "they will be banned for life." Indeed, the lifetime ban has been upheld in the courts.[2] However, many term-limited

---

[2]In *Bates v. Jones, Secretary of State of the State of California* (U.S. District Court Opinion, April 23, 1997), Judge Claudia Wilkens ruled that Proposition 140's lifetime limits violated the 1st and 14th Amendments to the U.S. Constitution. Her decision was ultimately overturned by an *en banc* panel of the 9th Circuit, and the U.S. Supreme Court did not take up the case.

legislators have continued their careers in the other house, in local office, or in statewide positions. Those who fought the initiative noted, "It raises new barriers to public office by banning our future representatives from earning any retirement except their current social security." We have not observed any shortage of people willing to run for office under the new retirement scheme, and many insiders report that new legislators are just as bright and qualified as before.

Opponents also predicted that if Proposition 140 passed, "lobbyists could substitute their own paid employees for the independent staff researchers." As nonpartisan staffing groups such as the Legislative Analyst's Office, the Senate Office of Research, and the Assembly Office of Research have been cut or disbanded, lobbyists appear to be more active in shopping bills and helping members round up votes. Yet we have no quantitative measures to record this behavior, which was not unknown before term limits. Finally, those fighting Proposition 140 claimed that it "upsets our system of constitutional checks and balances, forcing our representatives to become even more dependent on entrenched bureaucrats." Our examination of the relationship between the branches shows that the governor has gained power over the Legislature in budget negotiations and that legislative oversight of executive agencies has declined.

Although few of the most fervent hopes of Proposition 140's backers or the worst fears of its opponents have materialized, the initiative has dramatically changed California's Legislature. Many veteran legislators and staff members deeply regret what has happened to the institution to which they have dedicated their careers. Even the major figure behind Proposition 140, Pete Schabarum, recently voiced his discontent with the results. "What I was hoping was that we would have a group of 120 legislators who were actually private citizens willing to give a piece of their lives to public service. None of that is happening. It's become a partisan cesspool" (Sprague, 2004).

Coping with term limits means compensating for the problems that have arisen while recognizing the value of increased turnover and legislative diversity. Training is more important as relatively inexperienced legislators take on greater responsibilities. The appetite for legislator training is probably limited, but staffers play a more critical role than ever, making their training most essential. The budget process needs to be fixed as part of the structural remedy that will prevent a repeat of the deficits we have seen in recent years. The incentives to make a mark without dealing with the consequences are not good for fiscal accountability. We have recommended some changes to deal with this problem. Finally, the state should consider amending but not ending term limits by allowing legislators to spend their allotted 14 years in the Legislature running for office in either house.

Bibliography

Abrams, Matt, "Increased Amendments in California Make a Case For—or Against—Term Limits," *Institute of Governmental Studies Public Affairs Report*, Vol. 44, No. 1, Spring 2003.

Associated Press, "Lockyer Weighs Audit Requests on Quackenbush," April 4, 2000.

Barge, Liz, "Term Limits Affect Legislative Career Paths," *Institute of Governmental Studies Public Affairs Report*, Vol. 42, No. 3, Fall 2001.

Barone, Michael, and Richard E. Cohen (eds.), *The Almanac of American Politics 2004*, National Journal Group, Washington, D.C., 2003.

Bell, Charles G., and Charles M. Price, *California Government Today: Politics of Reform*, The Dorsey Press, Homewood, Illinois, 1980.

Block, A. G., and Claudia Buck (eds.), *California Political Almanac 1999–2000, Sixth Edition,* Statenet, Sacramento, California, 1999.

Bordetsky, Ann, and Lori Kim, "Unintended Consequences of Proposition 140: California's Legislative Oversight," paper for Political Science 171: California Politics, University of California, Berkeley, Spring 2002.

Brady, David, and Brian Gaines, "A House Divided? Evaluating the Case for a Unicameral California Legislature," in Bruce Cain and Roger Noll (eds.), *Constitutional Reform in California*, University of California Press, Berkeley, California, 1995.

Brokaw, Brian, Keith Jobson, and Paul Vercruyssen, "Knowledge and Power in the Post Term Limits Era: The Effects of Term Limits on Committee Chief Consultants in the California Legislature," paper for Political Science 171: California Politics, University of California, Berkeley, Spring 2001.

Cain, Bruce E., and Marc Levin, "Term Limits," *Annual Review of Political Science*, Vol. 2, 1999, pp. 163–188.

California Journal Press, *Roster and Government Guide,* Statenet, Sacramento, California, 2004 and earlier editions.

California Legislature, *California Legislature at Sacramento,* Sacramento, California, 1961, 1971, 1981, and 1989.

Clucas, Richard A., "California: The New Amateur Politics," paper presented at *Coping with Term Limits: Ohio and the Nation*, Columbus, Ohio, April 2000.

Congressional Quarterly's Who's Who in Congress, CQ Press, Washington, D.C., various years.

Department of Finance, *Race/Ethnic Population Estimates: Components of Change for California Counties, July 1970-July 1990*, State of California, Sacramento, California, July 1999.

Department of Finance, *Race/Ethnic Population Estimates: Components of Change for California Counties, April 1990 to April 2000*, State of California, Sacramento, California, March 2003.

Detwiler, Peter, "How Often Do Governors Say No?" California State Senate Local Government Committee, Sacramento, California, October 2003.

Ellis, Virginia, "Donations to Quackenbush Paid Wife's Campaign Debts," *Los Angeles Times*, March 26, 2000a.

Ellis, Virginia, "Quackenbush Rejected Steep Fines for Insurers," *Los Angeles Times*, April 2, 2000b.

Emanuels, Ken, Emanuels and Associates, "Ten Years into Term Limits: Academic Findings and the View from the Legislature," remarks at the Institute of Governmental Studies Conference, Sacramento, California, May 17, 2001.

Enemark, Dan, "Special Interests and Partisan Voting Patterns in the California State Legislature," paper for Political Science 171: California Politics, University of California, Berkeley, Spring 2001.

Enemark, Dan, and John Cross, "Term Limits Have Changed California's Legislative Behavior," *Institute of Governmental Studies Public Affairs Report*, Vol. 43. No. 2, Summer 2002.

Finnegan, Michael, "Ex-Governors Blame Legislature: The Former Leaders Say Term Limits and Safe Districts Contribute to the State's Political Dysfunction," *The Los Angeles Times*, February 18, 2004, p. B1.

Green, Stephen (ed.), *California Political Almanac 1991–1992*, 2nd edition, California Political Almanac Associates, Sacramento, California, 1991.

Grosedose, Tim, Steven Levitt, and Jim Snyder, "An Inflation Index for ADA Scores," *American Political Science Review*, March 1999.

Hodson, Tim, "Ten Years into Term Limits: Academic Findings and the View from the Legislature," remarks at the Institute of Governmental Studies Conference, Sacramento, California, May 17, 2001.

Huber, John D., and Charles R. Shipan, *Deliberate Discretion? The Institutional Foundations of Bureaucratic Autonomy*, Cambridge University Press, Cambridge, United Kingdom, 2002.

Jacobs, John, *A Rage for Justice: The Passion and Politics of Phillip Burton*, University of California Press, Berkeley, California, 1995.

Jacobson, Gary C., "Partisan and Ideological Polarization in the California Electorate," *State Politics and Policy Quarterly*, forthcoming.

Johnston, Patrick, "Ten Years into Term Limits: Academic Findings and the View from the Legislature," remarks at the Institute of Governmental Studies Conference, Sacramento, California, May 17, 2001.

Jones, Rich, "Ten Years into Term Limits: Academic Findings and the View from the Legislature," remarks at the Institute of Governmental Studies Conference, Sacramento, California, May 17, 2001.

Kang, Nancy, "Term Limits Shift Budget Bargaining Power," *Institute of Governmental Studies Public Affairs Report*, Vol. 42, No. 3, Fall 2001.

Kousser, J. Morgan, "Redistricting: California 1971-2001," in Gerald C. Lubenow and Bruce E. Cain (eds.), *Governing California: Politics, Government, and Public Policy in the Golden State,* Institute of Governmental Studies Press, Berkeley, California, 1997.

Kousser, Thad, "Term Limits and Legislator Performance," in Rick Farmer (ed.), *The Test of Time: Coping with Legislative Term Limits*, Lexington Books, Lanham, Maryland, 2002a.

Kousser, Thad, *Redesigning Democracies: How Term Limits Shape the Form and Function of State Legislatures*, dissertation, University of California, Berkeley, June 2002b.

Kousser, Thad, "Term Limits, Professionalism, and Legislative-Executive Conflict: Applying a Bargaining Model to the American States," paper presented at the 2002 meetings of the American Political Science Association, Boston, Massachusetts, 2002c.

Lee, Anka, "Term Limits May Generate Special Elections," *Institute of Governmental Studies Public Affairs Report*, Vol. 42, No. 3, Fall 2001.

Lucas, Donna, "Ten Years into Term Limits: Academic Findings and the View from the Legislature," remarks at the Institute of Governmental Studies Conference, Sacramento, California, May 17, 2001.

Lucas, Greg, "Quackenbush Brushes Off Growing Scandal," *San Francisco Chronicle*, April 12, 2000.

Masket, Seth, *A Party by Other Means: The Rise of Informal Party Organizations in California*, dissertation, University of California, Los Angeles, 2004.

Masket, Seth, "Building Better Partisans: What California's Experience with Cross-Filing Teaches Us About Party Effects," paper presented at the American Political Science Association meeting, Boston, 2002.

National Conference of State Legislatures, *Term Limited States by Year Enacted and Year of Impact*, 2004, available at http://www.ncsl.org.

National Conference of State Legislatures, *Elections Data Tables 1938–2000* [provided to author by NCSL staff].

Office of State Publishing, *California Blue Book,* Sacramento, California, 1950, 1954, and 2000.

Rosenthal, Alan, *Governors and Legislators: Contending Powers*, CQ Press, Washington, D.C., 1990.

Sanders, Jim, "Frenzy of Amendments Hits Capitol," *Sacramento Bee*, September 11, 2003.

Schabarum, Peter F., *Enough Is Enough: Term Limits in California*, SI: Modern Age Marketing Services, 1992.

Secretary of State, California, *Report of Registration, October 1986,* Sacramento, California, 1986.

Secretary of State, California, *Report of Registration, October 1996,* Sacramento, California, 1996.

Silva, Fred "Ten Years into Term Limits: Academic Findings and the View from the Legislature," remarks at the Institute of Governmental Studies Conference, Sacramento, California, May 17, 2001.

Sprague, Mike, "State Term Limits Show Progress, Fall Short of Goal," *Pasadena Star-News*, February 8, 2004.

Squatrigilia, Chuck, "Top Quackenbush Deputy Suddenly Resigns," April 14, 2000.

Van Vecten, Renee Bukovich, *Taking the Politics Out of Politics? State Legislative Term Limits and Institutional Political Reform in Twentieth Century California*, dissertation, University of California, Irvine, 2001.

Walters, Dan, "Ten Years into Term Limits: Academic Findings and the View from the Legislature," remarks at the Institute of Governmental Studies Conference, Sacramento, California, May 17, 2001.

Walters, Dan, "As Legislative Year Nears End, Major Bills Hatched in Semisecrecy," *Sacramento Bee,* September 10, 2003.

Wong, Christina, "In California, the Governor Has Become the Legislative Gatekeeper," *Institute of Governmental Studies Public Affairs Report*, Vol. 44, No. 1, Spring 2003.

Yang, Kelly, "California Legislative Giving Is Not Affected by Term Limits," *Institute of Governmental Studies Public Affairs Report*, Vol. 42, No. 3, Fall 2001.

Yang, Kelly, "Term Limits Get Too Much Credit for Boosting Female and Minority Representation," *Institute of Governmental Studies Public Affairs Report*, Vol. 43, No. 2, Summer 2002.

York, Anthony, "Bedlam by the Bay," August 1999, available at www.salon.com.

About the Authors

BRUCE CAIN

Bruce Cain is the director of the Institute of Governmental Studies and Robson Professor of Political Science at the University of California, Berkeley. A graduate of Bowdoin College in 1970, he was a Rhodes Scholar at Trinity College, Oxford, and received his Ph.D. in political science from Harvard University in 1976. From 1976 to 1989, he taught California politics, political theory, and comparative governments at the California Institute of Technology. He has served as a polling consultant for several State Senate races and as a redistricting consultant to the California State Assembly, Los Angeles City Council, and Attorney General of the State of Massachusetts. He has been a consultant to the *Los Angeles Times* and a frequent commentator for radio and television stations in Los Angeles and the San Francisco Bay Area.

THAD KOUSSER

Thad Kousser is an assistant professor of political science at the University of California, San Diego. His publications include work on term limits, reapportionment, campaign finance laws, the blanket primary, health care policy, and European Parliament elections. His book, *Term Limits and the Dismantling of State Legislative Professionalism*, is forthcoming from Cambridge University Press. He has worked for local, state, and federal campaigns and as a legislative aide in the California, New Mexico, and U.S. Senates. He received his Ph.D. in 2002 from the University of California, Berkeley, and his B.A. from Harvard University.

Related PPIC Publications

A California State of Mind: The Conflicted Voter in a Changing World
Mark Baldassare

California in the New Millennium: The Changing Social and Political Landscape
Mark Baldassare

The Season of Our Discontent: Voters' Views on California Elections
Mark Baldassare, Bruce Cain, D. E. Apollonio, and Jonathan Cohen

PPIC publications may be ordered by phone or from our website
(800) 232-5343 [mainland U.S.]
(415) 291-4400 [Canada, Hawaii, overseas]
www.ppic.org